D0431758

DON'T
PUSH
YOUR
PRESCHOOLER

OTHER GESELL INSTITUTE BOOKS

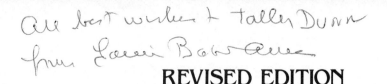

All best wishes & taller Dunn
from Louise Bates Ames

REVISED EDITION

DON'T

PUSH

YOUR

PRESCHOOLER

Louise Bates Ames, Ph.D.,

Associate Director, Gesell Institute of Human Development
New Haven, Connecticut

& Joan Ames Chase, Ph.D.

Formerly Clinical Psychologist, Children's Mental Health Center
Columbus, Ohio

HARPER & ROW, PUBLISHERS New York,
Cambridge, Hagerstown, Philadelphia, San Francisco,
London, Mexico City, São Paulo, Sydney 1817

Acknowledgment is made for permission to reprint the following material:

Excerpts from the book *The Black Child: A Parent's Guide* by Dr. Phyllis Harrison-Ross and Barbara Wyden. Copyright © 1973 by Dr. Phyllis Harrison-Ross and Barbara Wyden. Published by Peter H. Wyden, Inc., New York, N.Y. Reprinted by permission of the publisher. Excerpts from *Blueprint for a Brighter Child* by Brandon B. Sparkman and Ann Carmichael. Copyright © 1973 by Brandon Sparkman and Ann Carmichael. Reprinted by permission of McGraw-Hill Book Company. Excerpts from *Child Care and Development* by Louise Bates Ames. Copyright © 1970 By Louise Bates Ames. Reprinted by permission of J. B. Lippincott Company. Excerpts from "Children's Stories" by Louise Bates Ames. Copyright © 1966 by The Journal Press. First published in *Genetic Psychology Monographs,* 1966. Reprinted by permission of the Journal Press. Excerpts from an article by Dr. Anthony David that first appeared in the November, 1971 issue of the *Journal of Learning Disabilities.* Copyright © 1971 by Professional Press. Reprinted by permission of the Journal of Learning Disabilities. Excerpts from "My Life Story" by Sheila Greenwald. Copyright © 1966 by Harper's Magazine, Inc. First published in *Harper's Magazine,* July 1966. Reprinted by permission. Excerpts from *Teach Your Baby* by Dr. Genevieve Painter. Copyright © 1971 by Genevieve Painter. Reprinted by permission of Simon & Schuster. Excerpts from *William's Doll* by Charlotte Zolotow. Text copyright © 1972 by Charlotte Zolotow. Reprinted by permission of Harper & Row, Publishers, Inc.

Designer: Ruth Bornschlegel

Library of Congress Cataloging in Publication Data
Ames, Louise Bates
   Don't push your preschooler.

   Bibliography: p.
   Includes index.
   1. Children—Management.   2. Child psychology.
3. Readiness for school.   I. Chase, Joan Ames,
joint author.   II. Title.
HQ772.A47   1981   649'.123   80-8192
ISBN 0-06-010083-4

84   10 9 8 7 6 5 4 3

Contents

Acknowledgments

Thanks and great respect are due to Dr. Arnold Gesell and Dr. Frances L. Ilg, both of whom have in our opinion possibly contributed more to the science and understanding of child behavior than any other two individuals.

Their strong and consistent affirmation that "behavior is a function of structure" has perhaps done more than anything to combat the insistence of environmentalists that we can make any child into anything, and that how children turn out is almost entirely a result of what their parents have or have not done.

This book is also dedicated to the many good kindergarten and first-grade teachers who know they are getting many children too young, and who join us in urging parents—Don't Push Your Preschoolers.

Grateful thanks are due Mrs. Barbara Seaman and Mr. Arthur Hettich and *Family Circle Magazine* for instigating, publishing, and permitting the use of an article titled "Don't Push Your Preschooler," which served as the basis for the present publication.

Acknowledgments

Preface to the First Edition

Books which tell you how to improve your preschooler, how to make him smarter, speedier, more mature, abound. So-called stimulation of infants and preschoolers is now big business.

This book will suggest instead that you relax and enjoy what can be one of the most delightful times in the life of a family—the years when the children are very young.

But parenting is an art like any other. The more you understand this art, the more effective you can be as a parent. In fact, many high schools today are introducing courses in child care and development to help young people prepare for the sometimes demanding business of being a parent.

We do not think you need worry tremendously about trying to increase your child's intelligence or speeding up any of the abilities that will go to make up his total repertory. We do contend that the more you know about child behavior in general and about your own child in particular, the more effectively you can guide him through his preschool years.

It is our hope that the things we tell you here will help you as parents to be patient and relaxed but at the same time effective. As we shall point out, patience does not mean permissiveness. Relaxation does not imply rejection of responsibility.

Often the most successful parent is the one who seems to be taking things most easily.

Atlantic House
Scarborough Beach, Maine
August 10, 1973

LOUISE BATES AMES
JOAN AMES CHASE

1/ Don't Push Because . . .

The preschool years can be among the happiest and most satisfactory in any child's life, both for child and parents. Help keep them that way. Help your son or daughter to make the most of these years. Bringing up children can be fun. Don't spoil things for yourself and for them by expecting too much too soon or by trying to push them into behaviors for which they may not be prepared. It is not necessary to learn to count, read, or write in the first years of life.

Enjoy your child for what he is. Don't make yourself and him unhappy by feeling undue concern about things that *you* ought to be doing or that *he or she* ought to be doing.

This book will tell you some of the important things about preschool behavior that will help you understand your boy or girl. It will suggest some things you may like to do to make both your child and yourself happy and comfortable. It will also suggest some ways of behaving toward your child that in our opinion you might best avoid.

Keep in mind that the preschool years are a time for growing. We'll describe for you some of the usual stages that behavior goes through as the young child grows.

These years are a time for finding out what kind of person your young child is, and what kinds of techniques and responses and situations work out best for him and for you.

They are a time for learning—but the learning most important for the preschool girl or boy takes place in a three-dimensional real world, not in the schoolchild's two-dimensional world of pencil and paper.

Above all, the preschool years are a time for play. Let your child enjoy them. Parents today are being bombarded with advice and suggestions about ways in which, if they just do the right thing, they can make their children smarter and quicker and altogether more effective than they would have been without these special efforts.

"Maybe I don't spend enough time with him," "Maybe I ought to do more about teaching him to read," "Maybe I'm losing time when I just let him grow up naturally," are doubts that worry many young parents today. Even if you don't read the books that tell you how to increase your child's intelligence or how to raise a brighter child, there is a feeling in the air that parents ought to be doing something special about their children's minds.

We assure you, no matter what you read or what anybody tells you, it is not necessary for you to push your preschooler. There are several good reasons for this. The main one is

You Don't Need To

If you keep in mind that your children learn to walk and talk pretty much by themselves, it may help you relax about the other, more complicated things they're going to need to learn later on. Even when it comes to something as sophisticated as writing, John Holt, author of the popular *How Children Fail* (39), reminds us that learning to write, like learning to read, does not need to be a tremendously big deal.

He comments: "We should make it clear to children

that writing is an extension of powers they already have, and that they got for themselves, namely the powers of speech. We should constantly remind them that they figured out for themselves how to understand and talk like all the bigger people around them, and that learning to read and write is also easy."

Nature has her own intricate and highly effective plan and pattern. Nine months from the time of conception, without the mother having done much about it, except taking good care of her own health, a fully formed and fully functioning human infant is born with all its parts and possibilities.

After that, it takes a little more effort on the part of the parents. But just as the embryo and fetus develop through the complicated stages and changes needed to become an infant, so that infant goes through the stages needed to become a child, and the child goes through the stages that will eventually turn him into a full-fledged adult.

It is NOT all up to you.

If your boy or girl is normally well endowed, nearly all the important things he or she needs to learn in the preschool years will come about quite naturally. If your child is less than well endowed in any direction, what he will need is understanding, appreciation, encouragement, support, and help. The very *last* thing he will need is pushing.

It Doesn't Work

One of the best reasons for not pushing either the so-called cognitive development (thinking) of your preschooler or his other usual behaviors is that it doesn't work. To date, efforts to push preschoolers toward behaving in an either more mature or more intelligent manner than they might otherwise have done have been singularly unsuccessful.

Both research efforts, which have been extensive, and government efforts, which have been expensive, to raise the intelligence quotients of bright or not so bright children, or to improve the reading ability of the non-reader, have been disappointingly ineffective.

Furthermore, efforts to speed up the emergence of the various behavior stages have also been unsuccessful. Our own experimental efforts to speed up the behavior of babies, which we'll tell you more about in Chapter 5, convinced us that it was practically impossible, even with great effort, to speed up substantially the time of creeping, talking, walking, or handling objects.

It speaks well for American optimism that so many have so much confidence in their ability to push children along, farther and faster than Nature intended. It speaks less well for our good sense or our judgment, or our ability to learn from past experience.

Most parents do know that in spite of such things as little skating boards, which some companies provide so that you can put your baby on them and "teach" him to creep, babies do not creep until they are good and ready. They do not grasp objects in their fingers until a certain amount of physical maturing has taken place. If you think back to the fact that in most instances you were willing to wait for your *baby* to reach any desired stage of development, hopefully it will encourage you to continue to wait, within reason, till your preschooler's academic and intellectual abilities also make themselves evident.

Any Positive Effects of Pushing Are Seldom Lasting

"He's only five and he can read already. None of his cousins are that advanced." It gratifies some young parents to be able to make this boast. And many educators agree that it *is* possible by expenditures of considerable effort to encourage some small children to read somewhat ahead of the time when this ability would have come naturally and without encouragement.

The big question is, of course, whether it is doing the child any good to push him into early reading. Will it make him a better reader later on? If he reads better than the other four- or five-year-olds when he is four or five, will he read better than the other seven-year-olds when he is seven?

Sue Moskowitz, of the New York City Board of Education, some time ago reported studies that have not been contradicted. Her studies show that "the brightest two-thirds of a group taught to read early did not maintain their initial advantage over their classmates who had not learned to read before first grade."*

She also reported that a group of five-year-olds taught to read responded fairly well to this teaching but had forgotten almost all of it during the summer vacation. She tells of another study in which an investigator over a four-year period compared children who were required to begin formal instruction before six with those who started after six. These children not only made slower progress but did not develop as great a liking for reading as those who started later.

(Some children, of course, will spontaneously read early and should be permitted to do so. You should not hold children back from reading. No matter how young, the child, if he is turning out to be a naturally early reader, should be permitted to read. And such a child may very likely continue to read more advanced material than do other children of his age.)

The Scandinavian countries, believing as we do that there is really no great rush, do not as a rule begin reading instruction until children are seven years of age. (In fact,

*Paper read at the annual convention of the International Reading Association, Miami, Florida, May 1–4, 1963.

they do not begin children in first grade until they are seven.) Not only do Scandinavian boys and girls read as well as our children, but there are far fewer children there than in this country who experience reading problems and later need remedial help.

Such Efforts Not Only Do Not Come to Much but Often Lead to False Assumptions

Many optimistic adults, since the advent of *Sesame Street,* have come to the conclusion that children really are much smarter than we had thought, and therefore, once they have learned as preschoolers to say their letters and numbers, not only are smarter and quicker than preschoolers were in the past, but that the primary-school curriculum can also be speeded up.

The same notion was in the air a couple of decades ago when Omar Khayyam Moore started teaching preschoolers to read and type. He and his colleagues believed that as a result of their efforts most preschoolers could be taught to read and type, with the result that all our school curriculums could be accelerated. It didn't turn out that way. Certainly many responsible educators are working hard to improve school curriculums, but they probably will not succeed in having most children finish high school much earlier than at present.

People tend to take rote learning too seriously. They forget that a child who can recite his numbers to ten, or even twenty, still is often not able to perform even the simplest functions of arithmetic. A *Sesame Street* graduate who came to us recently with the proud boast (his mother's) that he could count to fifty, was still not able to write his numbers beyond a shaky three. He could not answer the question: "If John had four pennies, and his mother gave him two more, how many pennies would he have altogether?" because, as he explained, "I don't know John."

Your Child Is Busy Doing His Own Thing

Perhaps one of the chief reasons why you should not use great efforts to push your preschooler, especially not try to teach him to read and write and think abstractly, is that most preschoolers are very, very busy doing their own thing.

Professor Charles Wenar of Ohio State University, in his excellent book *Personality Development from Infancy to Adulthood* (74), points out that though sending a child to Sunday school can certainly have its advantages, it does not make him more moral. Morality needs to develop in its own slow way, as the child's increasing maturity makes it possible for him to understand what we mean by truth, honesty, and responsibility.

He emphasizes that "teaching academic skills to preschoolers, as so many advise, runs the same risks as teaching values. Undoubtedly many children CAN learn reading and other academic subjects before entering school. But knowing that a child CAN learn to read does not mean that he necessarily SHOULD learn to read, or that he is being deprived if he does not learn to read."

Professor Wenar asks how an emphasis on reading will affect other aspects of the child's development. He points out that dramatic play, not reading, holds the key to social relations in preschool. He suggests that "at the very least we should ask: During the time the preschool child is learning to read, what are the things he is NOT doing? In this way we can weigh what he is gaining against what he is losing."

Frank and Theresa Caplan, in their book *The Power of Play* (13), list the following advantages of play:

purposeful

Playtime aids growth. A child needs his early years of play to give him time to grow into the culture and into a readiness for formal learning. Play is a voluntary activity. It is intensely personal. It embodies a high degree of motivation and achievement. It is a happy activity beginning in delight and ending in wisdom. In his own play world, the young child is the decision maker and the play master.

Play offers a child freedom of action. It also provides him with an imaginary world that he can master. Play contains the elements of adventure.

It also provides an excellent base for language building. Vocabulary grows as the child plays. Play also has unique power for building interpersonal relations. The child explores not only the world of things in his playtime—he explores the ways that other children react to him. He finds out how far he can go with other people, what kind of approach serves best.

Play is the young child's world of sports. Older people play in formal ways and through games that have rules. Very young children learn, in play and without rules, ways of mastering the physical self. They climb, run, push, pull, and otherwise exercise large muscles. With tiny toys and objects they find out what their fingers can do and increase their finger skill.

And play provides a way for a child to investigate and practice adult roles.

So, what SHOULD your child be doing in his preschool years if he is not going to busy himself with learning his letters and numbers, as so many people nowadays advise?

He could be living and growing and playing, thinking and experiencing. He could be learning all about the world, the objects in the world, the people in the world, how to use his own body and mind effectively, how to interact with others.

There is a whole three-dimensional world of acting and doing to be explored and enjoyed. Time enough later on for the two-dimensional world of books, and of paper and pencil.

It Spoils Your Fun

A final important reason for not pushing your pre-schooler is that it spoils *your* fun. Possibly one of the greatest pleasures of parenthood is watching for your child's first steps, listening to his first words, or even earlier, admiring those first occasions on which your new arrival takes hold of some part of the world around him with eyes or hands.

If you are content to wait and go along with Nature, you will be just as happy and excited when your baby starts to creep, or to pull himself up in his playpen or crib, at eleven months as at nine or ten. You will be as well satisfied if he pat-a-cakes at forty-four weeks as if he had done it at forty. You will be as well content, though this may be a bit more difficult, if he manages to stay dry at two and a half years of age as if he had managed this big achievement at two.

Nature, more often than not, knows what she is doing. Almost every new and usual behavior develops through a series of small, orderly, predictable steps. Creeping behavior, alone, develops through a series of more than twenty intricate, interesting, patterned stages. How much fun to know a little something about the way usual behaviors develop, and to watch and enjoy their gradual, more or less inevitable, unfolding! How much fun and how much more relaxing than to set your heart on the final stage of any kind of behavior, and then to push and fret in what will in all likelihood be fruitless efforts to speed up a child's individual, inborn timetable.

The danger or disadvantage of pushing is that if you are busy thinking about what you are trying to *make* your child do, you lose the pleasure of enjoying what he *is* doing, without any major assistance from you.

How much more comfortable to let your child make his own timetable, especially since, for all your efforts and ambitions, that is in all likelihood the one he will follow anyway.

Perhaps it may help you relax if, for a minute, we think about something as basic and as un-anxiety-provoking as your baby's teething. Though the first tooth of one's first child or grandchild admittedly can provoke a good deal of excitement (how could he do that all by himself?), admittedly after the first (child or tooth), most people take the whole process of teething rather calmly (unless, of course, it hurts, and the baby cries).

Most reasonable parents have every confidence that their baby's teeth will come in, in plenty of time, *and with no special help from mother or father. Try if you can to feel equally relaxed about behavior.* Believe with us that behavior to a very great extent is a function of structure. When your child's body and brain have reached a certain stage, with only reasonable and minimal help from you and the rest of the environment, appropriate behavior *will* make itself evident.

There are, of course, many things you can and will want to, and need to do, as this book will tell you. But one thing you do *not* need to do is to push your infant or preschooler in what almost certainly will be a vain attempt to make him or her quicker or smarter than Nature intended.

2 / Why Do People Push?

So why *do* people push their preschoolers?

Some push because they are *ambitious*. They want their children to succeed and excel, and believe that their own strenuous efforts can bring about exceptional academic and intellectual success.

Some push because they are *conscientious* and feel it is their responsibility to make very special efforts.

Some push because they are *misinformed* and actually believe those psychologists and educators who assure them that they really can and must do something very unusual and out-of-the-ordinary which will result in increasing their child's intelligence, and accelerating his academic performance.

From the earliest days of our country's history, our children have enjoyed infancy, played through early childhood, and then, hopefully, gone on to academic or practical success without too much prodding.

There have always been a few pushy parents, parents who took great personal pride and satisfaction in the supposedly superearly and superremarkable achievements of their young. "Only ten months old and walking already." "Talked in sentences before she was a year old." "Completely toilet-trained long *before* her first birthday."

Such boasts, whether true or not, obviously gave a great

deal of satisfaction to those who uttered them. However, most parents today have seemed willing and able to live their own lives, get satisfaction from their own accomplishments, and permit their children to grow at their own natural pace.

How, then, if this is true, have we suddenly arrived at a point where many parents *are* pushing their children, many educators are leaning on even preschool children in an effort to develop their "cognitive abilities," and some psychologists are claiming that even infants can be speeded up in their behavior development, if only one does that beautiful, right thing?

It's hard to narrow down to a single point, but the current tendency to push infants and young children toward ever speedier performance *may* have started with Sputnik. All of a sudden we were not the first and the best, and something *had* to be done about it. Schools started beefing up their curriculums, and many insisted that even infancy and the preschool years should not be wasted.

It was during this Sputnik era that some child specialists conceived the notion that if we could start academic teaching earlier than currently was the custom, and thus no longer "waste" those precious preschool years, we could speed up the entire course of education.

Thus, if we could teach three- and four-year-olds to read and type, they would be ready for the usual work of first grade a year or two earlier than at present. This would make six-year-olds ready for second or third grade (at least), and would permit boys and girls to graduate from grammar school, high school, and eventually college at much earlier than the customary ages.

Such efforts attracted much attention and interest, but predictably did not come to much. One graduate of such a program, in retrospect, remembers her childhood experience in the O. K. Moore program:

THE LIFE STORY OF A MODERN FOUR-YEAR-OLD
MY LIFE STORY BY SHEILA GREENWALD

From the day I was born, my parents have seen to it that I am a winner. When I was two years old, I was taken to a cubicle in New Haven where they taught me to type. Two-year-olds can learn such things, and if they don't, they merely waste their time.

When two-year-olds who don't know how to type meet two-year-olds who do know how to type, they are overwhelmed and fall behind and are losers from then on.

At two-and-a-half, I was sent to school, where I play with learning equipment. I excel in carrot grating. My playtime is not frivolous or wasted. I learn about textures and colors and relationships. At three my mother taught me to read. Children of three can learn to read and if they don't, they waste their time. They fall behind in school from the start and they are losers.

My parents never neglected the social side of my development. I have been exposed to children constantly. After school I attend play group. Relationships with one's contemporaries cannot start soon enough and are vital in the child's development. If these exposures to one's contemporaries don't begin soon enough, the child cannot cope with them when he starts grade school. He falls behind. He is a Loser.

I began to attend rhythm classes at three-and-a-half. I play drums and run like a pony, which strikes me as somewhat frivolous, but it instills something in me they say and I'll be a winner rhythmically speaking.

Now that I am four, I feel sure of my ground. When I enter the kindergarten of my choice in the fall, it will be with a sense of purpose and readiness to cope with all situations. I will be on my way as a winner.

When I grow up I would like to be a garbage man.

Even with the dreadful possibility facing us that the Russians might stay ahead of us, many parents, educators, and child specialists have remained calm. They did not feel that teaching our babies to read, or instructing our six-year-olds to put out little newspapers, was absolutely necessary to maintain our national honor. Those who remained calm were for the most part the more biologically oriented individuals who believed, more or less, that not only the quality and quantity of an individual's potential, but even the rate at which he might be expected to develop, were to a large extent biologically determined.

Even the most biologically oriented individual does admit that there is *interaction* between organism and environment, and that one must, inevitably, be provided with a good if not ideal environment in order to achieve his top potential. Thus Dr. Arnold Gesell, who is accused by some of ignoring the environment and of thinking that it doesn't matter, in 1942 commented specifically, "Environmental factors modulate and inflect but they do not determine the progressions of development."*

Even earlier he cautioned, "In appraising growth characteristics, we must not ignore environmental influences —siblings, parents, food, illness, education. But, the organism always participates in the creation of its environment. The growth characteristics of the child are really the end-product of an *interaction* between organism and environment."†

However, anyone who is biologically oriented accepts the fact that even the best environment cannot make of any human being more than the top of what his inherited nature makes possible. On the other hand, extreme environmentalists actually appear to believe that almost anybody can be made into almost anything if only one works

*Arnold Gesell, "Documentation of Infant Behavior in Relation to Cultural Anthropology." In *Proceedings of the 8th American Scientific Congress, Anthropological Sciences,* 2 (Dept. of State, Washington, D.C., 1942), pp. 279–91.

†Arnold Gesell, "The Stability of Mental Growth Careers." In "Intelligence: Its Nature and Nurture," Chapter 8 of *Thirty-Ninth Yearbook of the National Society for the Study of Education,* Part II (Bloomington, Illinois: Public School Publishing Co., 1940).

at it hard enough and starts soon enough. Not only this, but some consider it *wrong* for anyone even to propose that what a person may turn out to be is to any extent determined by heredity.

As Roger Williams puts it:

Those who worked in the so-called Behavioral Sciences rather ridiculously invited the biological sciences to stay *out* of the precinct of human behavior. The opinion-makers of two generations have literally excommunicated heredity from the Behavior Sciences. This neglect of the study of heredity has effectively produced a wide gap between biology and psychology. . . . The idea that it is ALL a matter of education and training cannot possibly be squared with the hard biological facts of inborn individuality.

The current perversion of education (insisting that if done right, education can make everybody alike) perpetuates the banishment of heredity from our thinking. But we must face the fact that biologically each member of the human family possesses inborn differences based on his brain structure and on his vast mosaic of endocrine glands, in fact in every aspect of his physical being.*

And *The American Psychologist* points out: "The history of civilization shows many periods when scientific research and teaching were censured, punished or suppressed for seeming to contradict some religious or political belief. . . . Today a similar suppression, censure, punishment and defamation are being applied against scientists who emphasize the role of heredity in human behavior."†

In the past few decades an extreme environmental point of view, one which tends to belittle or even deny the role that heredity plays in determining how able and intelligent a child may be, or how fast he may be expected

Saturday Review, January 30, 1971, pp. 17–19.
†July 1972, p. 660.

to develop, has definitely dominated in both the psychological and the educational worlds. The press has reflected this atmosphere, and thus parents have, inevitably, been influenced in the direction of feeling that they not only *can* but *should* teach, push, hurry, and mold their children in the directions in which they would like to see them develop.

All through this era the biologists, though often unheard or even scorned, have consistently maintained that behavior is a function of structure, and that to a large extent how fast your boy or girl develops, the direction he (or she) will take, and how far he may go, though influenced by what you may do for, with, or to him, will be primarily determined by the body and brain inherited.

As Yale psychologist Edward Zigler has so aptly put it:

Not only do I insist that we take the biological integrity of the organism seriously, but it is also my considered opinion that our nation has more to fear from unbridled environmentalists than we do from those who point to such integrity as one factor in the determination of development. . . . It is the unbridled environmentalist who emphasizes the plasticity of the intellect, who tells us one can change both the general rate of development and the configuration of intellectual processes which can be referred to as the intellect, if we could only subject human beings to the proper technologies.

In the educational realm, this has spelled itself out in the use of panaceas, gadgets and gimmicks of the most questionable sort. It is the environmentalist who suggests to parents how easy it is to raise the child's I.Q. and who has prematurely led many to believe that the retarded could be made normal, and the normal made geniuses. It is the environmentalist who has argued for pressure-cooker schools, at what psychological cost we do not yet know.*

_____

*"The Nature-Nurture Issue Reconsidered: A Discussion of Uagiri's Paper," paper read at Conference on Sociocultural Aspects of Mental Retardation, Peabody College, Nashville, Tenn., June, 1968.

Whatever the reasons, and they clearly are multiple, we have in the past decade been inundated with books which tell you how to improve your child's mind, how to make him or her not only smarter but more mature than would have been the case if you did not intervene in some very special way. Some of these books contain sensible suggestions for good ways to play with, or work with, the very young child. Their fault, in our opinion, is that they tend to promise rather more than they can perform. And they tend to make some parents feel that if children can be made brighter and more adequate by special efforts, they are remiss not to be making these efforts.

It has become the fashion these days to believe that it is a parent's responsibility to work with infant or preschooler for the purpose of developing his mind. Our countersuggestion is that you should relax and enjoy those earliest years with your child. Help him do things that are easy and comfortable for him at his stage of development. Don't worry about speeding him along at a rate faster than his maturity level permits. Do not worry about improving his mind.

It seems safe to say that if you are a reasonably advantaged mother or father, the chances are that you are quite naturally, and without anybody advising you, doing many or most of the things you need to do to see that your preschool boy or girl will grow up to be as bright and effective as his genetic inheritance intended him to be.

Obviously you will do what you can to help him enjoy life. Fortunately, the ordinary things that the ordinary, effective parent does in relation to his infant and child tend to be quite sufficient to allow that child to express himself at least *toward* the utmost limits of his genetic potential.

The things many or most of the advice books tell you you should do for and with your very young children (you SHOULD teach them to pat-a-cake; you SHOULD encourage them to creep and walk; you SHOULD show interest when they speak; you SHOULD play little games with them as they develop) are things that most parents have always done as a matter of course.

Less-advantaged mothers and fathers, young parents who themselves did not have too much of a chance, and who even now that they are parents may find life very difficult, may be too harried, hurried, and harassed to give more than the very minimum of time, attention, and effort to the children they have produced. They may appreciate basic instruction about even rather simple aspects of home-making, such as that given in *Teach Your Baby* (55): "The home should be run in an orderly manner so that each member of the family knows that there is an over-all schedule and that certain things happen at a regular time. A regular time for meals, nap, play and bedtime is essential."

If a parent's background *has* been sparse, if his own parents didn't talk to him, play with him, be with him, read to him, plan for his present and future—then it is admittedly possible that one or several of the many books that tell you what to do may be helpful.

The hazard of all these books is that the majority of parents in this country (parents who themselves have had a fairly normal childhood and who *do* enjoy their children and spend time with them) get the feeling that there is something *more* that they should be doing than all those many lovely, lively things they do quite naturally.

If you are a parent who has had even a reasonably stimulating childhood, if you love and enjoy your infant and child, if you listen to him and respond to him, you really don't need a book to tell you how to do the simpler things. And, above all, you will appreciate the fact that Nature has her own timetable. This will tell your boy or girl (and you) when he or she is *ready* to talk, walk, read, write, or engage in abstract thinking.

There's no question that infants and young children need and benefit from a great deal of give and take with parents and others. This give and take, obviously, is going to be most pleasurable and most effective if it fits the level of the child's own interests and abilities. Pat-a-cake demonstrations are not going to mean very much to a two-month-old infant or to a three-year-old child. But around nine or ten months, when the adult pat-a-cake fits what the ordinary child is just naturally doing (bringing his two hands together), pat-a-cake is going to be the hit of the day.

You don't need to be self-conscious and anxious about your child's mental or intellectual development. But there are good and reasonably easy things you *can* do to help him (and yourself) get the most out of his preschool years. Some of those things are included in the chapters that follow.

3 / What You CAN Do: Know What to Expect

That we urge you not to push doesn't mean that you should just sit back and do nothing where your preschoolers are concerned. Far from it. In bringing up any child there is a tremendous amount that you *have* to do and a lot more that you can do if you wish.

A book titled *Blueprint for a Brighter Child* (69) tells you about many things you can do, supposedly, to sharpen your young child's thinking. We're not so sure about that.

But there IS a blueprint that is important for you. It is a very exciting, and, we believe, helpful, blueprint that tells you how the young child's behavior develops. The architecture of growing behavior is amazingly complex and intricate, but at the same time its basic structure is easy to understand. Understanding this structure can be of tremendous help to you in knowing what to expect from the young person you are raising.

As children grow older, they grow bigger and more capable. But they do not necessarily become better-behaved or easier to get along with. Just because a child is older and in many respects more able by no means implies that life with him or for him will be easier and more comfortable than when he was younger.

"All of a sudden," parents tell us, "he became impossible."

Then they quite naturally look around for reasons to

explain this sudden change for the worse in their formerly perfectly good child. "Jimmy's never been the same since he had whooping cough when he was around two-and-a-half. He was such a gentle child before that." "Bill was terrific until he started school, but he has been very hard to handle ever since." "Her grandmother spoiled her that winter she lived with us. Pammy's been a different girl ever since that visit."

Gradually, however, as the study of child behavior progressed and the professionals became involved, it became evident that there was some rhyme and reason to these all too frequent changes for the worse. (Changes for the better were less often noted or commented on. People seemed to take them for granted.)

The first formal description of behavior swings from good to bad appeared in 1943 in *Infant and Child in the Culture of Today* (30). This book emphasized the fact that behavior at any given preschool age amounts to more than the sum of the specific things that a child is able to do. Each age is characterized by its own special qualities of behavior, which seem to hold for a majority of children of that age.

Not only does each age seem to have its own special characteristics, but a basic theme of development seems to run through all ages. In general, ages of what we may call equilibrium alternate rather systematically with ages of disequilibrium. Ages when behavior is expansive and sure alternate with ages when it is close to home and much less sure.

Many parents have found this concept useful in explaining why, all of a sudden, their calm, compliant two-year-old becomes difficult and defiant, contradictory and compulsive at two-and-a-half. It helps them understand what is going on when their gentle, friendly, calm and comfortable three-year-old suddenly seems insecure and demanding at three-and-a-half, or when that same three-

and-a-half-year-old suddenly becomes bold and defiant at four.

If such changes are seen simply as characteristics of aging, and not merely due to the fact that grandmother came for a visit and "spoiled" him, or that he "learned" all those wild ways from the other children at nursery school, a parent may feel under less compulsion to cure or change an environment that supposedly was having such bad effects on a presumably "good" child.

Certainly, one does not just let undesirable behaviors continue on the grounds that they represent "normal" growth stages. Any parent, no matter what he or she "knows," will undoubtedly prod and punish, shape and mold, reward and resist, as parents always have. But many report feeling calmer about sudden and undesirable turns for the worse in behavior if and when they realize that their child "is not the only one." Somehow, even unattractive or undesirable behavior is a bit more acceptable when one knows that in all probability it does make sense from a growth point of view, and also that it will probably change with further growth.

Patterned swings of behavior between inwardized and outwardized behavior, between equilibrium and disequilibrium, do, we believe, take place in infancy as well as in the years that follow. But it may not be too useful for parents to know about them. This is because behavior changes very rapidly in infancy, and also because individual differences in timing are very great.

Thus it is true, for instance, that a time of rather marked disequilibrium does *on the average* take place around thirty-two weeks of age, whereas just earlier (twenty-eight weeks) and just later (thirty-six weeks) *on the average* behavior is calm and smooth. But if your own baby should be just two or three weeks ahead of, or behind, this average schedule his disequilibrium could come at thirty weeks, or at thirty-four. Individual variations are so great and changes so rapid that some parents find it more confusing than helpful to think too much about small age changes in infancy.

Most parents we have known find that a knowledge and understanding of typical behavior swings and changes is of most practical value at and after eighteen months of age, by which time behavior changes more slowly and gradually and what is going on can be more easily identified by the parent.

We shall explain later in this chapter that although any given boy or girl may be somewhat ahead of or somewhat behind any expected norm, many children do seem to express a marked stage of disequilibrium around eighteen to twenty-one months of age, followed by good equilibrium at two, disequilibrium at two-and-a-half, equilibrium at three, disequilibrium at three-and-a-half. Four tends to be an age of marked expansion, which may provoke disequilibrium in the adult but which the child seems to enjoy. Five years of age is often an age of both equilibrium and inwardization.

Eighteen Months

Eighteen months is an extremely interesting halfway station between infancy and early childhood. The mother who said of her eighteen-monther, "You have to program him as if he were a robot" was perhaps speaking correctly. Certainly the wide variety of choice that the older child experiences is not available to the eighteen-monther. There are only a certain number of things that he can do. He is limited by his very immaturities in his choice of how he will behave.

If it sometimes seems that your typical eighteen-monther is rather difficult, and hard to please, remember that he is quite as difficult for himself as for you! He has difficulty because he cannot entirely count on his own person to perform as he might wish it to.

Thus the usual eighteen-monther cannot yet choose to be fleet on his feet.

Motorwise he is coming into many new abilities of locomotion, but they are still at an all too tender stage. He *can* now walk upright unaided, can even run, after a fashion. But he is never safe from falling because his ability to walk is still so new. And though he loves staircases—would happily bumble up and down for minutes at a time—his speed is reduced by the necessity of using two feet to a step.

For all that posture may still be rather awkward, and coordination not too certain, the eighteen-monther *loves*

BEHAVIOR SWINGS BETWEEN POOR ADJUSTMENT AND GOOD ADJUSTMENT

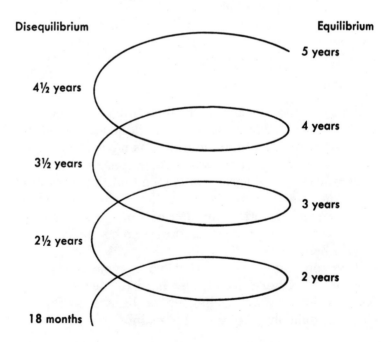

Disequilibrium   Equilibrium

5 years

4½ years

4 years

3½ years

3 years

2½ years

2 years

18 months

motor activity. Watch him as he lugs, tugs, dumps, pushes, pulls, pounds, moves furniture, pulls his beloved pull-toy. Gross motor activity still predominates over fine motor. He can grab and push and pull, but as yet he cannot manage those fine motions of wrist and fingers that will soon make delicate manipulations a success and pleasure. He still uses whole arm movements in ball play or in play with a doll or toy animal.

Languagewise he definitely cannot count on himself. There is much that he wishes to say, for which he just does not have the words. How frustrating to want the blue bib instead of the pink and not to have the word for "blue"!

Emotions are still unstable. Emotional expression he has, and plenty, but it is not well modulated. The eighteen-monther, if he does not like sight or situation, cannot yet merely restrain himself to a frown or pout. Rather, he is all too likely to put on a full-fledged temper tantrum over what may actually be only a minor frustration.

Perhaps most difficult of all, for him and for you, is the fact that it is extremely hard for him to adapt his actions to your demands. We have described the typical eighteen-monther as walking down a one-way street. And that street tends to lead in the direction opposite to the one you had in mind.

Thus he typically says "no" instead of "yes," "won't" instead of "will," "down" instead of "up." All this makes the child of his age more than a little difficult to deal with, though even his kind of definition by opposition marks a new maturity compared with the time when he was but one year old and on a more positive beam.

The eighteen-monther almost seems to think with his feet. He does not think ahead to what he is going to do. Rather, he runs around almost at random, stopping to investigate briefly whatever he comes into contact with. This in contrast to the older child, who moves purposefully toward an object of his choice.

The child of this age is largely motor-driven. It is almost as if one winds him up and then he functions. Thus the adult in charge must do quite a bit of his thinking for him, and must not expect too much rational action from him.

His attention span is still remarkably short. Because his interest shifts so quickly, it may be hard to keep him entertained, but he also quickly forgets his objection to some activity or routine. Thus, if you can shift his attention even briefly from something that is giving trouble, often you can return rather quickly and with success to that same activity.

Other people: Though he may be temporarily responsive to his parents and other adults, the typical eighteen-monther is not yet much interested in other people. To a large extent he ignores other children, or treats them as objects, poking at their eyes or pulling at their hair—not in anger or hostility as much as by way of exploration. Or he may grab an object from another child with little attention to the child grabbed from.

Though his most used word in conversation with others tends to be "no," he may also say "hello" or "'bye," or may show and name a real or pictured object, spontaneously or in response to encouragement from an adult. Or he may ask for something he wants by pointing and using his familiar "eh eh." He does on occasion, and if so moved, respond positively to simple, clear verbal directions from the adult.

Techniques: The biggest error that parents of the eighteen-month-old child tend to make is in thinking of him as more capable than he actually is, or in deciding that it is now time for him to *mind.* Now that he is mobile and talking, many parents assume that they need merely tell their child to "Come here, dear," and he will or should do just that. Not so, as experience will show.

Thus, at this point, if not earlier, you begin to use *techniques.* You adapt your handling to the child's immaturity. Discovering that he does indeed walk down a one-way street, and that that street does tend to go in a direction other than the one you have in mind, you refrain from counting too much on "Come here, dear." If you need to have the child where you are, there are several ways of getting him there *if* you will but reckon with his immaturity.

You can go up behind him, lift him up, and move him to where you want him to be. You can hold out a beloved toy, or a cookie, or any other enticing object. Or you can turn your back and crackle a piece of paper or make some other interesting noise. He will come to find out what it is that you are doing. There are *many* indirect ways to persuade an eighteen-monther to do what you want him to. Just find some stimulus that attracts.

Perhaps your best clue to the management of the eighteen-monther is *not* to expect him to do things to please you. *Do* expect him to do things that please him. Knowing your own child, you can quite easily discover those things that will lure him from one place to another.

For the child who loves outdoors, just the word "out" may be all that is needed. Or if he associates his hat with a walk outdoors, you can say, or produce, "hat."

Once outdoors, he may bumble into every byway, want to pick up every fallen twig. Urging him to hurry is not good motivation. Walking away from him backward, for some reason or other, makes you attractive to him, and chances are he will come running.

He may very likely resist being touched or having his arm held (even when he darts dangerously out into the street) but many will accept a harness if it is used only when needed. The harness should be used with a loose rein except when needed to break a fall. The reins can be looped up when not needed.

In the house, the success of the child's play, at this age, depends largely upon the *presence* of interesting playthings and the *absence* of hazardous equipment. Because the eighteen-monther is a furniture mover and is beginning to be a good climber, it is wise to remove chests or drawers and small tables and chairs that he can move while he is playing in his room. If a chest of drawers remains, the drawers should be locked to keep him from getting into them. Or his dresser *could* be turned to face the wall. Windows and screens should be securely fastened.

Toys that are too difficult to handle, and thus bring on crying, or toys that offer any hazard whatever, should be permitted only when adults are present. Books, which the child is likely to tear, should not be left available, though you may be willing for him to play with (and tear) discarded magazines. Light plugs should be either disconnected or covered over, because of the danger of an electric shock resulting from the child's inserting sharp metal objects.

Valuable or breakable objects of your own should so far as possible be removed from reach. This is not the age to teach the child to MIND, or to LEAVE THINGS ALONE. Much less energy will be required, and much greater success attained in this direction, when he is just a bit older. At this time you will merely end up frustrated and unsuccessful.

This is not the age at which you will successfully decide, "It's high time now that he does so and so." High time or not, if his body and brain are not ready, you are not likely to succeed. Great patience and a wise assessment of what he IS ready for will save you a great deal of time and trouble.

A full-fledged temper tantrum is the eighteen-monther's way of telling you when things go wrong or when he has had enough. Most parents find that the best way to combat a tantrum is, if at all possible, to ignore it. Better still is to know your child and the limit of his endurance well enough that to a large extent you can divert or support when things are going just too wrong, so that you prevent the tantrum before it occurs.

One of the best possible techniques, if and when a tantrum threatens, is distraction. Let's say you are putting your eighteen-monther into his highchair at mealtime and he stiffens out and refuses to fit into the chair, and then goes on to wave his arms and scream. Do not continue stuffing him into the chair. Instead, give up this project for the moment. Let him get down onto the floor and then distract him in some interesting way.

You might let him go to the refrigerator and select some bit of food that looks good to him. Or you might clown around and get him to join you in a dance or jig. Neither honor his refusal by entering a contest with him, nor make an issue of his behavior. Help him forget that he did not want to sit in his chair and have lunch. A second attempt, without any special emphasis on what you are doing, is likely to be met with no opposition whatever.

Discipline as we usually think of it is not the important thing at this age. It is not necessary yet to make the child obey you in the conventional sense. It is more important, by whatever means you can, to arrange just to get him through his day.

In general, you will see that the chief techniques effective with an eighteen-monther are gross and physical. You control him by controlling his surroundings, and by not having too many things around that will get him into trouble. Or you control his activity by a harness, or simply by picking him up and putting him where you want him to be, without words and with no big fuss. Language in general is not (as it will be later) his best motivator. And if you do use language to motivate him, *keep it very simple and use words of one syllable only.*

Two to Two-and-a-Half Years Old

The typical two-year-old tends to be rather a gentle, friendly little person, much easier to live with than he was a mere few months ago. Life is easier than it was, for many reasons.

To begin with, he is much surer of himself *motorwise* than he was just earlier. Now he can walk and run and climb with rather admirable skill, so that the world of movement is a comfortable one for him.

Now he can *talk*, so very much better than he did at eighteen or twenty months. Not only can he express his needs better, but since TWO is a somewhat gentle, undemanding age, these needs are not as strong as they were. This happy combination—diminished needs and a better ability to express himself—makes it easier for the child to get what he wants from the world. This makes life more fun for him, and makes him more fun for the adult.

Emotionally he seems calmer, surer, better balanced. Anger and disappointment are not as strongly felt as formerly, nor as strongly expressed. Also, emotionally, the child seems to be, at least briefly, on the positive side of life. He likes other people, and they in turn find him a delightful companion.

The age of TWO provides a brief and welcome breathing space for a parent, coming as it does between the difficult, demanding time of eighteen to twenty-one months and the even more difficult and demanding age of two-and-a-half. Unfortunately, it is as if the child cannot function always on the positive side of life. Stages, or ages, when things are fine and in good equilibrium seem to need to break up and be followed by stages when things are not so fine and equilibrium is not as steady.

Two-and-a-half years is a time of opposite extremes. By his very nature, the child of this age has merely to choose *red*, and he wants *blue*; to choose *yes*, and he wants *no*.

At eighteen months, the typical boy or girl walks down a one-way street, and his direction tends to be the *opposite* of the way *you* have directed. Now he has matured to the point where he sets up his own opposition. He makes a choice and that very choice motivates him to try its exact opposite. This is how he finds out about the world —by exploring both of any two opposite extremes in quick succession. Irritating as this kind of behavior may be to the adult, it is a very important part of growing up.

A second strong and striking characteristic of the two-and-a-half-year-old is his demand for sameness. He wants everything to be always the same. It is not just the order in which things are carried out, or the way they are done, that must be the same; it is the place they occupy. He wants everything in the household left right where he put it.

Place requirement may extend to an insistence on always taking the same route to nursery school or to other familiar destinations. The world is large and confusing to the child of this age. A consistent route gives him orientation and confidence.

Time, too, must be programmed, in order for him to feel comfortable. If Father usually comes home just before supper, and on one particular day Father comes home early, your two-and-a-half-year-old will still expect supper to follow immediately after Father's appearance. His time is *event* time, not clock time.

The two-and-a-half-year-old, above all else, is bossy and demanding. "King John," "Queen Julie," mothers often say. The child is bossy not because he is sure, but actually because he is unsure. For the two-and-a-half-year-old the world is big and dangerous. If he feels that he can command even a small part of it (his parents), it helps him to feel confident. His "Me do it myself" should at least on occasion be respected.

Relationship with others is not easy. In associating with

other children, one rule seems cardinal in the mind of the two-and-a-half-year-old. This is that he is going to hang onto and defend any toy he has played with, is playing with, or might play with. His possessions are almost a part of himself, and to give up anything is highly painful to him. "Mine" is still a key word with him.

Things are much more important to him than people, and his wish to do anything in order to please others is minimal. He himself is, to his way of thinking, the one to be pleased. The two-and-a-half-year-old has relatively little interest in his contemporaries.

Life is complicated, too, by the fact that the child of this age finds it extremely difficult to wait or to take turns. His attention span and his waiting span are a little bit better than at eighteen months, but not much better.

Knowing all this, you will pattern your guidance accordingly. You will try not to think of the child as "good" or "bad," as "generous" or "ungenerous," as "co-operative" or "unco-operative." Rather, you will set up those situations, or give those directions that will help him use his extremely immature and unpracticed social abilities most effectively.

Thus a see-saw does take two to play. Clay play, with plenty of clay for everyone, or side-by-side painting with separate easels and sets of paints, can encourage rudimentary social behavior.

Since children themselves have so little ability to adapt to the demands of others, much help from an adult will usually be needed. It will help considerably, when John demands to have the tricycle that Jerry is playing with, to say to John, *"When he's finished,* you can have it," or to say to Jerry, "It will be *his turn* pretty soon."

A magic word at two-and-a-half is NEEDS. Many a child has been known to relinquish a prized possession if a mother or teacher will just whisper to him, "But Billy NEEDS it." (This of course works two ways. When he

Gesell Institute

THE ROCKING BOAT ENCOURAGES GROUP PLAY

himself NEEDS something, he, too, expects to receive it.)

Techniques: Take advantage of the child's ritualism. Do this by setting up rituals of your own to get him through the rough spots of the day. A good bedtime ritual may include—first undress, then bath, then pajamas on and teeth brushed, then a swing on a doorway swing, then go to the bathroom, then bed and a certain number of certain bedtime stories, then a hug and good-night kiss, and then lights out.

Accept your child's need for sameness. So far as is practical, permit his toys and other possessions to stay where he puts them, furniture in the household to remain where he expects it to be.

Accept and even welcome the security measures he sets up for himself, as his favorite blanket or toy, or his own thumb. They may be lifesavers if you find it necessary to travel or to move. Even in strange surroundings, a small bit of security can mean a lot.

Even as earlier, you protect the child from his own lack of inhibition—it is still hard for him not to grab at forbidden or attractive objects—by what we label "household engineering." Put your most valuable or breakable objects where he cannot reach them. Or by means of gates or other barriers, keep him out of the more fragile parts of your house. This is not lack of discipline or giving in. It is common sense. When he is a little older and his own inhibitors are a little stronger, "discipline" will be easier for you and more effective.

Give face-saving (your face) commands as much as possible. Try not to trap yourself in some inflexible demand such as "You have to pick up all your toys before you can have your dinner." Far better to suggest, "Let's pick up the toys now." Then, if he absolutely refuses to take part in the pickup, you will not be stuck with trying to push through an order in which you may, before the situation has terminated, have lost all interest.

Good face-saving techniques include:

Say, "Let's do so and so," and then if need be, you can do the major part of the work.

"How about doing so and so?" is also good. If his answer is "No," so be it. You can give up on the whole thing without embarrassment.

"Where do the blocks go?" when it's pickup time may motivate the child to put them where they belong. If he doesn't, no matter.

A good face-saving technique, *after* a child may have refused, is to make a joke or some humorous remark. Or change the subject, or leave the scene completely.

For best results, do what you can to bypass the rigidities of the two-and-a-half-year-old. Try to avoid head-on clashes about whether he will or will not do what you want him to. Chances are that he will not, and if you insist on meeting resistance head-on, *you* are apt to be the loser. Instead, divert him when you can from what is going on.

Thus, if your child does not like to get dressed, try to avoid big arguments about whether he will or will not allow you to put his clothes on him. Instead, set him up on some rather high surface and dress him quickly, all the while talking rapidly about some future happening.

Try to avoid giving the child of this age a peg on which to hang his opposition. If, for instance, he wants to do something that will not be appropriate till later, avoid the dangerous word "later." It will merely activate his own "now," and you may find yourself engaged in a tiresome and fruitless game of "later," "no, now," "later," "no, now."

Instead, if it must be later, say something like "O.K., we'll do that, but first let's do this or that." You elaborate cheerfully and positively until (hopefully) he may entirely forget his original demand. Or at least you may have stalled him along till actually it *is* later. If a request cannot be granted, distraction of any kind may be your best bet.

If you find yourself involved in one of those fruitless "I want—I don't want" routines, in which the child demands some toy, food, article of clothing, or activity, and then the minute he gets it, rejects it, and then when you take it away wants it again, it may be impossible to resolve the situation at his level. You will need to break into his impasse. This is best done by terminating the situation and shifting to entirely different ground. You can do this by leaving the scene, taking *him* away from the scene, or introducing some entirely new object or idea. You have to help him break into his own tendency to shuttle between opposite extremes.

Sometimes a child can be motivated by giving him a

choice (about *unimportant* matters): "Do you want the red one or the blue one?" Questions that can be answered by "no," such as "Do you want your supper now?" should be avoided if it is important to you that the answer be "yes."

Three to Three-and-a-Half

As a rule "good" ages alternate with "bad"; times of equilibrium alternate with times of disequilibrium; and periods when behavior tends to be expansive and outgoing alternate with periods when everything seems to be pulled in.

Thus it should come as no surprise to the mother of a rambunctious two-and-a-half-year-old that sometime around the age of three her son or daughter does seem to calm down conspicuously. He says "yes" instead of "no," "will" instead of "won't." He smiles instead of frowns, laughs instead of cries, gives in comfortably to requests instead of resisting them.

And, then, just as you are really beginning to enjoy this tractable little creature, growth forces push your child's behavior a little further along in its ever-evolving cycle, and he hits three-and-a-half, a wild and wonderful age with characteristics all its own.

You may not need much help and advice when your child is three. When he is three-and-a-half you may need all the help you can get and then some.

We may fairly, and in all friendliness, describe the three-and-a-half-year-old boy or girl as being characteristically inwardized, insecure, anxious, and, above all, determined and self-willed. One might assume that his strong-willed self-assertiveness, which is so conspicuously evident, might be rooted in a strong personal security. Not so! In fact, the very opposite seems to be the case.

The three-and-a-half-year-old child seems to feel extremely insecure. This insecurity is evidenced even in physical ways. He stutters. He trembles. He stumbles. A child who six months earlier may have walked a proud one foot to a step up the stairs may now go back to a more babyish two feet to a step. Quite steady at three, he may now express his fear of falling. Steady-handed at three, as he built a sturdy tower of blocks, his hands may now tremble as he adds blocks to his tower. Handedness may even shift at this age and it may seem as if the child actually did not know which hand to use.

Tensional outlets of all sorts are conspicuous at this age. The child may suck his thumb, bite his nails, pick his nose, blink his eyes, rub his genitals, chew at his garments. And he may well hang onto his security blanket as if onto life itself.

Emotional insecurity as well as physical insecurity is commonly expressed at this often difficult age. The three-and-a-half attempts to control his environment in ways that will, perhaps, make him feel more secure. "Don't look," "Don't laugh," "Don't talk" he commands those around him. But, in his immaturity, he is inconsistent. "Don't look," he may order at one minute, and at the next insist that ALL attention be focused on himself. He may refuse to let Father read his paper or Mother do her housework, or allow Mother and Father to talk to each other.

Inconsistent, and determined to control the adult, he can make things difficult, since he must have his own way about everything. And he is surprisingly firm in enforcing his demands. If, while out for a walk, he decides that he will not go any farther, he will stand stock still. If you walk away, assuming that your departure will motivate him to follow, you can continue on till he is but a speck in the distance. He will not budge.

Or he will set up a "nothing pleases me" situation in which, as when taken shopping, he does not want to go into the store but at the same time refuses to stay in the car, and will howl bloody murder whichever alternative you choose.

But it is routines that tend to give the greatest difficulty. During the smoother parts of the day, between routines, he may be loving and amusing—his most delightful self. He can indeed be warm, friendly, appealing, affectionate, confiding, imaginative, creative, and delightful. It is hard for you to imagine that only minutes before you and he may have been locked in mortal combat over whether he would or would not eat his lunch.

This is an age when friends are very important. The usual three- or three-and-a-half-year-old plays rather well with other children. It is easier now for him to take turns and share, and he enjoys co-operative play. "We" is a favorite word. Friendships are tremendously important, and it is in their play with others that one often sees children of this age at their most charming and best. Many now enjoy the company of imaginary companions—either people or animals. One boy we knew had a whole family of imaginary bears.

One further delightful aspect of behavior at this age is the child's increasingly effective verbal ability. Not only does vocabulary continue to increase, but the child now uses language as an interesting means of real communication.

Techniques: As at every age, the very best techniques you can use are tailored to fit the strong points, and the weak ones, of the age itself. When the child of three-and-a-half tends to be VERY hard to handle, it is important to keep in mind that your child is not your enemy. Those times when a child is at his *worst* are the times when he needs the *most* from you. He is not behaving as he does just to be naughty. He is behaving as he does because that is the way his organism functions at this time of life. He really cannot help being the way he is, so it is *you* who must help him.

So, what can you do to help things go smoothly for both of you?

First of all, accept the fact that at this age the child's big emotional struggle is with his mother. She is the one who matters supremely to him. She is the one he needs to conquer. Almost any young child is at his best, but also at his worst, with his mother. Never more so than now.

Recognizing this, a mother or another person in charge, will if at all possible enlist the services of a good baby-sitter for as much of the day as possible. It may be somewhat deflating to see an untrained high school girl lead your son or daughter smoothly through routines that you, the parent, cannot manage. But that is the way it is.

Why? Because the sitter really does not care, deeply, if your child fails to eat a good meal, dress properly, go to bed quickly. The three-and-a-half fights ONLY with a worthy opponent—YOU.

And once you are away from him, try to stay away. If the sitter has him out in the yard for the morning, do not keep appearing. If you have managed to get him down for his nap, do not appear at the door (or window). The mere sight of you may start up unnecessary problems.

We recommend that you enjoy to their fullest those moments between routines when your child may be fun to be with. Enjoy your play with him, since he will, if permitted, very much enjoy his play with you.

If you are ingenious enough, some master plan can solve an entire problem area over a long period of time. Instead of enduring daily battles over some bit of the day's routine, try to find some big solution that will solve more than the immediate incident.

With her early waking and strong demands for parental company, one little girl we knew was a daily disaster to her mother and father. They solved the problem by providing an early morning "surprise," such as, for instance, a few raisins or peanuts. If she played quietly and enjoyed the surprise without disturbing them, her reward, in addition to the food, would be praise from her parents. And there would also be another surprise next day. That took care of the early morning, with only the rest of the day to go.

Remember that television can be your friend. It can keep a child contented and out of difficulty, and if you supervise your child's viewing, its effect should not be harmful.

If mealtimes are difficult and no baby-sitter is at hand, you may find it easiest to provide as best you can and then tell your child, "There it is," and leave the room. Otherwise, every bite may be a bone of contention.

Serious fights over dressing can be diminished by letting the child keep his T-shirt on overnight, and/or providing pajamas that button in the back, thus reducing "over-the-head" problems.

If your child is one who all of a sudden becomes quite unmanageable in stores or out on a visit, try to keep such outings to a minimum. FOUR will love and profit from excursions with you. Three-and-a-half may be better off at home.

If you are one whose child enjoys an imaginary companion, you can sometimes encourage him to do things "nicely" in order to set a good example for his companion. If he is one who pretends that he has a kitten, you may find that "kitten" will quite willingly and graciously do things that your son John habitually refuses.

Needless to say, if your child is still hanging onto his security blanket at this age, you will make the most of it. Anything that quiets him and makes him more docile should be fully exploited and appreciated.

As at two-and-a-half, you will, if wise, continue to use

face-saving techniques. It is not essential at this time to prove that you are your child's master. It is more important that you and he (or she) get through the day as friends, or at the very least with nerves not too badly frazzled.

So make heavy use of "How about—," "Let's—," "Maybe you could—." Use any phrase or any technique that will permit you and/or your child to withdraw gracefully from a situation in which he finds himself unable to comply with your command.

Absolutely refuse to let yourself get mixed up in the preschooler's favorite game of "I don't love you." Just refuse to become emotionally tyrannized by expressions of affection or disaffection. In his need to control his parent, the child of this age will use emotional threats IF they work. See to it that they do not. At the same time, don't use love or the withholding of love against him, since he is extremely vulnerable to the threat of not being loved, at this age.

The emotions of the child of three-and-a-half tend to be rather fragile. He may express many fears, and especially visual fears of people of unusual appearance, of the dark, of animals. Within reason it is best to protect him, or at least to support him, when he is fearful. Do not be ruled by his fears, but do not, when they are at their height, force him to face the things he fears.

One very troublesome fear that some three-and-a-half-year-olds express is a sometimes almost hysterical fear of having their parents go out in the evening. Though no parent likes to be controlled by his child's demands, it may be kindest to keep evening absences at a minimum while this special fear is at its height.

Whatever the anxieties and demands and frustrations of the three-and-a-half-year-old, or of being the parent of a child of this age, try to keep in mind—this too will pass.

Four Years Old

The four-year-old is a funny little fellow, and if you can accept him as such, you can have a very good time with him. If, on the other hand, you take a sterner stance and feel that his boasting, his swearing, his generally out-of-bounds behavior is *wrong*, or a prelude to later delinquency, both you and he may have a quite unnecessarily hard time of it.

We have found the boy or girl of this age to be for the most part joyous, exuberant, dynamic, ridiculous, untrammeled—ready for anything. What a change he offers compared with his more difficult, demanding, three-and-a-half-year-old earlier self! If at times he seems somewhat boastful and bossy, it is because it is so exciting to enter into the fresh fields of self-expression that open up for him at this wonderful age.

The child at three-and-a-half characteristically expressed a strong resistance to almost anything the adult required, possibly because to him the adult was still all-powerful. FOUR has taken a giant step forward. All of a sudden, he discovers that the adult, though still quite powerful, is not ALL-powerful. He finds much power now in himself. He finds that he can do quite bad things, from his point of view, and the roof does not fall in.

More than this, following its seemingly built-in policy of interweaving, Nature sees to it that whereas the three-and-a-half-year-old was much of the time rather withdrawn and insecure, FOUR is on the expansive and highly sure-of-himself side of living.

Combining this expansiveness with his exciting need to see just how far he can go before the grownups call a halt, the four-year-old generously expresses what we consider the outstanding characteristic of his age—his love for going out of bounds.

A normally vigorous and well-endowed child of this age may seem out of bounds in almost every area of living. He not only hits and kicks and spits (if aroused) but may even go so far as to run away from home if things don't please him. Whether he is happy or not, his motor drive is very high. He races up and down stairs, dashes here and there on his trusty tricycle.

Emotionally, too, he tends to be extremely out of bounds. He laughs almost too hilariously when things please him; howls and cries more than too loudly when things go wrong. He can, on frequent occasion, be extremely silly.

But it is his verbally out-of-bounds expressions that sometimes upset the uninformed adult most. He boasts: "I have bigger ones at home"; "I can do better than that." There is all too frequent reference to garbage: "You're doing that all wrong. If you do it like that, I'll cut you up and throw you in the garbage." Adjectives and nouns tend to be on the unacceptable side: "Stinky"; "Wee-wee"; "Pee-pee." There are all too frequent lapses into profanity: "Jesus Christ!" is a frequent expletive. Or the child may criticize the adult with epithets and threats: "You're a rat"; "I'll sock you."

Not content with unacceptable language, all too many a four-year-old departs from the truth to an extent that any literal-minded adult can think of only as prevarication. (It is important not to call the child a liar, since the label may stick long after the behavior has disappeared.)

Exuberance, of course, has its positive side. The typical four-year-old LOVES adventure, loves excursions, loves excitement, loves ANYTHING new. He loves new people, new places, new games, new toys, new books, new activities. No one is more responsive to the adult effort to entertain. He will accept what you have to offer with delightfully uncritical enthusiasm. Thus it is a pleasure to provide him with new toys, books, clothes, experiences, because his eyes sparkle so, because he is so wholeheartedly appreciative.

This is a period of enthusiastic acquisition of new facts, new fancies, new interests, and new abilities. The child seems almost consciously trying to be grown up. (Witness his love of dressing up in adult clothes.) It can be a real pleasure to help him, and to take part in his growing.

Four is an extremely friendly age. Children now enjoy the notion of "friend," and a nursery-school teacher can often stimulate a friendship simply by announcing to a child that "here is your friend who wants to play with you."

FOURS are not as rigid about interpersonal relations as they were just earlier. Quarrels or disputes tend to be quite easily solved. For the most part, four-year-olds find each other of great interest, so that as a rule play goes reasonably well.

Techniques: Perhaps the best way to calm the child down, when some of his wilder ways—his profanity, his boasting, his supersilly talking—bother you, is to ignore him. "He only does it to annoy" the old rhyme tells us. So, if you show him that you not only are not annoyed but that you do not even notice, the thrill of profanity or exaggeration goes down, in most, rather quickly.

An opposite technique, and one which is more fun and perhaps equally effective, is to join in and enjoy. You will not enjoy his profanity, but you can often enjoy his exaggerated stories by countering with your own, obvious, exaggeration. A lion chased him home from school? Two lions chased you. He is silly? You can be more so. And certainly you can join in with and truly enjoy some of the wonderfully silly poems and stories now available for four-year-olds.

FOUR loves new adventures. Share them with him. Create them for him. A simple trip around your own neighborhood, with its inevitable points of interest, takes on new luster for you when seen through the enthusiastic eyes of a four-year-old. And when you plan an excursion, plan it with him in mind. A short walk, perhaps past a spot where a new building is going up (or better still being torn down), and an ice-cream cone on the way back will be a lot more satisfactory to a four-year-old than a cultural expedition to a nearby town.

Since the child of this age does tend to go out of bounds, you will need, for safety, to find the most effective way of containing him within what you consider to be acceptable limits. Environmental restrictions, such as gates or closed doors, are not as effective as they were earlier, but most at this age do respond pretty well to verbal restrictions such as: "as far as the gate"; "as far as that tree"; "as far as the corner."

Since this is an age when children love "tricks" and new ways of doing things, sometimes, if a child balks or stalls, you can motivate him by suggesting that he "hop" or "skip" toward some desired destination.

Transitions do not present the difficulty that they did some six months earlier, but if there is trouble with transitions this can often be countered by enthusiastic talk about the next proposed activity.

Happily, many four-year-olds respond very adaptively to the stricture, "It's the rule." They may not even question why.

Children of this age tend to be insatiably curious. Try to answer their "whys" as long as you feel that real curiosity and interest motivate them. Don't hesitate to cut the conversation short when the whole thing gets out of hand.

Since FOURS love exaggeration, in your efforts to motivate or restrain, as well as in your efforts to entertain, you will find exaggeration to be very effective. "As high as the sky," or "in a million years" work well. Or just plain silly language as "mitsy, bitsy, witsy," or "goofy, woofy, spoofy," can often interest or distract, when distraction is needed.

Take advantage, freely though carefully, of one of the great new things society has to offer for the preschooler —television. All of a group of four-year-olds recently studied by us did watch television, most having three or four special programs. Preschool favorites do not change very much over the years. *Captain Kangaroo* remains an outstanding favorite, followed by *Mister Rogers, Sesame Street, Electric Company, New Zoo Review, Bugs Bunny, Tom and Jerry, The Flintstones,* and, of course, the Saturday morning cartoons.

Television can be one of your best devices for meeting FOUR'S high demand for excitement, activity, and drama.

Once you appreciate what a child of this (or any) age is like, it helps you to appreciate what he *will* like. You can tailor your techniques accordingly.

Four into Five

Now just a word about that interesting transition time —four into five.

We know that the typical four-year-old girl or boy tends to be extremely exuberant, enthusiastic, outgoing, out-of-bounds. We also know that at five* the same child will in all likelihood be calm, collected, quiet and self-contained, adaptable, conforming, well adjusted, easy to get on with, happiest and most comfortable while engaged in conservative, close-to-home activities.

How does he get from four to five? The transition tends to be rather gradual. Sometimes the child himself seems confused, as if he really does not know whether he is a

---

*For full information on five and the years that follow, you may like to read Gesell and Ilg, *The Years from Five to Ten* (New York: Harper & Row, 1977).

wild four-year-old or a calm and quiet five. Adults often find the child's behavior, at this time, highly unpredictable.

A clue to the uncertainty of four-and-a-half is his strong interest in whether things are "real" or not. Making a REAL drawing of an airplane, he may include an electric cord so that people can plug it in. "Is it real?" is a customary question.

At four-and-a-half the child tends to be a bit more self-motivated than he was just earlier, and he tends to stay on the job better than he did. Children of this age are interested in gathering new information and in perfecting old skills. Play is less wild than at four, and most are better able to stand frustration. But emotions may be quite uncertain. Laughter and tears follow each other in quick succession.

All in all, four-and-a-half is an unpredictable age. But if you keep in mind where the child has been and where he is going, it can sometimes help you to define where he is now.

4

What You CAN Do: Know Personality

"Mike has so much *energy!* And he's so loud! He's not a bit like my other children. It just seems as if he is physically unable to walk quietly, talk softly, sit still. Of course I like the children to show a certain amount of zip—but he's too much."

"My Julie is just the opposite. I wish she would show a little more enthusiasm. She is so quiet you'd hardly know she was in the house. And she doesn't seem to have any friends, doesn't seem to care about other children. All she really wants to do is stay in her room and read."

"I guess I'm lucky with Betty. She is SO satisfactory. Just doesn't seem to have any trouble or give me any trouble. She's warm and friendly and affectionate. Everybody loves her. I worry a little that she is a bit overweight, but that's because she loves to eat."

Three children in three different families. But they could all three be in the same family since, as most of you know, brothers and sisters do not always resemble each other and in fact may not even resemble their parents. Admittedly, some differences in personality and behavior do result from the way family, and the world, treat any child. But probably the basic differences that occur are based on the fact that different children have different bodies.

For hundreds of years some students of human behavior have observed that human bodies come in different shapes as well as sizes and that people's behavior is related to the kind of body they have.

Constitutional psychology, as this theory is called, suggests that children—and grown people for that matter—behave as they do to a very large extent because of the way their bodies are built. The popular notion that fat people in general tend to be friendly, muscular people tend to be athletic and active, and thin people tend to be sensitive and shy, has long been held by many to be based on a certain amount of truth.

Yet the notion that we are not entirely free to behave as we wish, and not entirely free to make our children turn out as we wish, is a hard one for many Americans to accept. As Margaret Mead remarked, only if we should find that we can *change* the body type will the study of physical differences as determining behavior become popular in American society.

There are two important beliefs underlying our own study of human behavior. One is that behavior changes in a patterned way with age. This notion has become well accepted by parents all over the world. People often write and tell *us* about it. But its correlate—that behavior is a function of structure and that to a large extent an individual's behavior depends on the kind of body he has inherited—has been less popular and harder for many people to accept.

In spite of the fact that we, and others, have written about this subject frequently, the basic idea that to a very large extent we can tell what children are and will be like, what they can and cannot be expected to do, as a result of the fact that their bodies are built in one way or another, has never been fully accepted and used by the majority of parents and teachers. Yet we believe it can help you to understand your own children better than you now may.

So here, in brief summary, are a few of the basic facts or possibilities about human behavior based on physical structure, which we expect will be helpful to parents of preschoolers. The sooner you recognize and accept your child for what he is, the sooner you can help him to be a good whatever he is. The longer you delay such recognition, the more likely you are to waste effort and energy and even emotion in trying to push a child into being something that Nature never intended (and very likely will never permit).

Many of us have been taught by our own parents that "looks don't count." It is true in a sense. People with extremely even, beautiful features are not necessarily more intelligent or more moral or otherwise more deserving or desirable than people with uneven features. But, in a more important sense, looks DO count.

The child with the soft, rounded, well-padded body (whom Dr. William Sheldon classes as an *endomorph*) may be expected to behave quite differently from the stocky, broad-shouldered, squarely built, well-muscled *mesomorph,* or from the thin, angular, flat-chested, and stoop-shouldered child with pipe-stem arms and legs whom we call an *ectomorph.*

Physical Appearance

In a little more detail (Sheldon, 61; Ames, 2), people of the three physical types differ as follows:

The body of the endomorph is round and soft; of the mesomorph: hard and square; of the ectomorph: linear, fragile, delicate. In the endomorph, arms and legs are relatively short compared with the trunk, with the upper part of the arm longer than the lower part. Hands and feet are small and plump. Fingers are short and tapering. In the mesomorph, extremities are large and massive, with upper arm and leg equal to lower arm and leg in length.

Hands and wrists are large, fingers squarish. In the ectomorph, arms and legs are long compared with the body, the lower arm longer than upper arm. Hands and feet are slender, fingers are fragile with pointed fingertips.

Many parents find it both interesting and helpful to try to figure out which of these customary body type classifications best fits their own child or children, and to what extent his or her behavior fits our expectations for people of that body type.

Knowing how endomorphs or mesomorphs or ectomorphs customarily behave, or are thought to behave, may help you to fit your own expectations closer to reality than might otherwise be the case. Obviously, the more closely your expectations agree with reality, the happier and more comfortable both you and your child will be. Many parents find themselves quite ready and able to accept some less than ideal child behavior if they feel secure that this is the way their particular child may be expected to behave.

It is important to keep in mind that most people do not fall entirely in one category or another. Most have some characteristics of each. But in most people one or the other tends to predominate. Thus, for practical purposes, we may speak roughly as if each child were of one type or another.

Here's something else it may help you to know. According to Sheldon, the endomorphic individual is one who attends and exercises *in order to eat.* Eating is his primary pleasure. The mesomorph, on the other hand, attends and eats *in order to exercise.* What he likes best is athletic activity and competitive action. The ectomorph, on the other hand, exercises (as little as possible) and eats (with indifference) *in order to attend.* Watching, listening, thinking about things and being aware are his most enjoyable activities.

Sheldon gives another good clue to the differences

among the three types. He says that when in trouble the endomorph seeks people, the mesomorph seeks activity, while the ectomorph withdraws and prefers to be by himself.

Now all this is not just a matter of theory. Endomorphs, mesomorphs, and ectomorphs behave very differently from each other in the ordinary situations that make up everyday living. Here are some of the things you may expect of your own boy or girl, depending on his physical makeup.

Eating

The typical *endomorph* loves food. He may almost be said to live to eat, and he will eat almost anything. Even when not eating he likes to be doing something with his mouth as chewing gum, sucking a lollypop, or enjoying a nice soft drink. Mealtime is seldom a problem with such a child, except that he may tend to eat too much, too often.

The *mesomorphic* boy or girl is less enthusiastic about food but still tends to have a big appetite. If you do not, by your insistence on certain specially disliked foods, spoil things, the mesomorph, as a rule, does not give too much difficulty in the food department.

Not so with the *ectomorph.* Mealtimes for him may be the hardest time of day. Appetite tends to be very, very small, and even the mere sight of a plate heaped with food may turn off what little appetite he has. Color and texture of food may also turn him off. He may refuse to eat anything mushy, or lumpy, or of the wrong color as, for instance, "those little green balls" (peas).

The ectomorph can live and thrive on much less food than most parents think he needs; and five small snack-meals a day might suit him better than the three large ones customary. Don't push him, and he will as a rule comfortably decide on his own nutritional needs.

Sleeping

The *endomorph* not only loves to eat but as a rule also loves to sleep. He snuggles down contentedly with his thumb or teddy bear, and enjoys nap or night sleep, lying limp and sprawled in almost any position.

The *mesomorph,* as a rule, also is a good sleeper. He drops off to sleep quickly and easily, sleeps soundly though often with much thrashing around. He often seems to need less sleep than do other children, and he is one who wakes quickly and easily, jumps out of bed and then wakens you, cheerfully, at 6 A.M. or even earlier.

The *ectomorph* has trouble with sleeping as with eating. He finds it hard to get to sleep, but once asleep, finds it hard in the morning to wake up and get going. He needs a great deal of sleep, but it is hard for him to fall asleep unless he is close to physical exhaustion. He sleeps lightly and dreams a great deal. That is, his relaxation, even in deepest sleep, is incomplete.

Reaction to Other People

The *endomorph* loves company. He is warm and friendly with others. He likes people and people like him. They tend to feel relaxed and comfortable when they are with him. He does not, even as a young child, like to be alone.

The *mesomorph* likes people, too, but he is nowhere near as dependent on their company as is the endomorph. However, he usually has plenty of friends and is a natural-born leader even in his preschool years. He likes people well enough, but as a rule other people have to adapt to *him.* He gets on best as a leader or as the one the others look up to. He likes others primarily because of the things they can do, because of the activities they can enjoy together.

The *ectomorph,* in contrast to the other two kinds of

child, has a strong need of privacy. He likes to be alone and dislikes to be socially involved. If he has a choice—which the young child does not always have—the ectomorph avoids being too much involved with other people. He tends to be distressed, uncomfortable, anxious and shy in social relationships, as in nursery school, where he relates better to the teacher than to the other children.

Emotions

In this respect as in others, unless we know our own child well and know what it is reasonable to expect of him and what his behavior really means, we are apt to misjudge him. It is important for parents to know that the typical *endomorph* expresses his emotions fully and freely. He may cry as if his heart would break but then get over it quickly. He is easily comforted with kisses and hugs. Loud howls do not necessarily mean that he is in great difficulty.

The *ectomorph,* even as a very young child, finds it much harder to express his emotions. He may suffer deeply without shedding a tear. Parents and teachers need to keep an eye on him, since it may be hard for him to show when he is in trouble. If he does break down and cry, especially in nursery school, it may embarrass him deeply. It is difficult to comfort him because it is hard for him to accept physical comforting.

He is the child who minds terribly if he does not get his "turn," but may find it extremely difficult to ask for a turn. He needs more help and support emotionally than do other children.

Things are quite different with the *mesomorph,* who may be characterized as one whose emotions are best expressed in his love of power. He loves to compete, to dominate, to command, to conquer. He has great push, drive, and energy. He is *not* sensitive to the feelings of others, and seems himself almost insensitive to pain. He is courageous and likes to lead. If angry or upset he tends to take it out on somebody, usually his mother or a younger sibling.

Problems

Here are some of the things that cause parents the most anxiety about behaviors characteristic of children of different body types:

The *endomorph,* typically jolly, friendly and well adjusted, does not as a rule pose any great problem to his parents. As a baby such a child is usually described as unusually "good." He eats well, sleeps well, and seems to love life. As he grows older, he gets on well with most everybody. He is a nice kind of child to have around.

If parents, too, are of this temperament, there is not much to worry about. But if parents are more driving, more competitive, more ambitious, then they do tend to worry that their endomorphic child does not try hard enough, does not compete. They consider him lazy and even in the preschool years his lack of drive may cause them (not him) anxiety. Try to accept the fact that great drive and extreme good nature seldom go hand in hand.

The *mesomorph,* on the other hand, especially in the preschool years before he learns to channel his great energy into acceptable lines, can be a great source of anxiety to his parents. He tends to be constantly active, into everything, highly destructive. His hands must touch everything he sees, and he seems to break nearly everything he touches. His mother is worn out just trying to keep up with him, and he easily earns the reputation of being "the worst child in the neighborhood." Though he usually gets on well with contemporaries (he bosses them around and is looked up to as a leader), he tends to lack sensitivity and thus may be hard to reach. One thing that makes him a lot of trouble to adults is that he is so very loud and noisy.

He needs much opportunity for active play, especially outdoor play. He needs somebody strong and tireless to play with him. He needs adults who enjoy rather than suffer from his displays of boundless energy.

The *ectomorph* causes anxiety for quite another reason. As a baby he is likely to suffer from colic and other feeding disturbances. He also often has sleeping problems. He may have more than his share of allergies. What worries parents most, however, is his oversensitivity, his social shyness, his immaturity, and the fact that he may not seem to need people. All these things combine to make it hard for him to find friends. Keep in mind that this kind of child needs time alone. He needs people who understand his quietness and shyness. He especially needs parents who will not push him into athletic and social activities for which he may be unsuited.

Understanding Your Child for What He Is

If you have been blessed with an *endomorph,* enjoy his warmth and friendliness. Don't push him too hard. He may never be a real go-getter, but if you can accept him for what he is, you and he will both be happy.

With your energetic, trouble-prone *mesomorph,* since spanking and corporal punishment may have only momentary effect, concentrate more on supervision and on providing legitimate outlets for his boundless energy. Try not to "see" everything that happens. You cannot punish him for every "bad" thing he does—there will be too many. Praise him for the good things he does in order to encourage him to repeat them.

Try to keep your equilibrium, protect your property and your child from physical harm, and see that you have some relief every day (school or baby-sitter). Keep in mind that the mesomorphic drive which makes so much

trouble now may in later life lead him to great success.
Get as many secure locks as possible to protect medicines and any other dangerous or fragile items in your house. Put other things as high as possible.

Give this child a good supply of things to be messy with —clay, dough, paint, sand, water, soap. Also provide as much equipment as possible for outlet of gross motor energy—a jungle gym, bouncing board, doorway swing.

And now for the *ectomorph*. How can you best help him? One thing is to keep in mind that this boy or girl, though often quite bright, matures slowly. Don't worry about this or about his lack of social success. Later on he may catch up with or even surpass, in some ways, those who got an earlier start. But most of all, and this is especially important for fathers, let this kind of child know that you like and appreciate him even if he is not athletic and outgoing, even if he is diffident and shy, even if very small things that go wrong seem to bother him unduly.

A final warning about body types. In trying to figure out your own child's physical type it is important for you to remember that people are not *all* one thing or another, but rather they are a mixture of all three components described. It is just that unless a child is unusually well rounded, one component or the other (endomorphy, mesomorphy, or ectomorphy) tends to predominate and in all likelihood will have the most influence on what he or she will be like.

It may surprise and interest many of you to learn that not only do many child specialists believe that they can to quite an extent predict how a child will behave from an observation of what his body is like, but that there *are* those specialists who believe that distinctly individual characteristics appear in the human individual even before birth.

There is a new science called *fetology* which studies and attempts to care for the human baby before he is born. Dr. Margaret Liley, a New Zealand fetologist, tells us, in her book *Modern Motherhood* (51), that "in treating the unborn, we have found that the human fetus possesses distinct characteristics from about the fourth month of intrauterine life, before his mother even feels him." Dr. Liley considers the fetus to be a unique individual, with distinctive characteristics and responses to external stimuli. She considers him to be an active, not a passive, partner in the pregnancy itself.

She assures us that "once the baby is started there is very little we can do about the kind of person he will be. We do not breed the children we want. *We must accept what we get.*"

This chapter thus far has presented the following ideas: behavior is to a large extent a function of structure; a child's behavior can to quite an extent be predicted and understood from an observation of his physical body; and differences in structure—and thus in personality potential —are observable even in earliest infancy.

In considering all these things, we urge all parents— *don't try to push your child into being something or somebody that his body does not permit.* Certainly you should not sit passively by. You can smooth down rough edges and help your child play down personality characteristics that give him and others trouble. You can, conversely, help your child play up his good points. You can try to "bring out" the shy child, but you cannot even by your greatest efforts push any child into being a totally different individual from the one he was born to be.

There are, of course, many ways of thinking about and classifying personality other than in relation to body build. Thus Dr. Stella Chess of the New York University School of Medicine, in *Your Child Is a Person* (14), suggests that we think of children in terms of the following eight classifications: activity level, regularity, adaptability to changes in routine, level of sensory threshold, positive or negative mood, intensity of response, distractability, persistency. You may find it helpful to think of your own child in terms of these categories.

But whatever terms or classifications you use in trying to understand your child's basic inborn individuality, it is obvious that he will not be growing up in a vacuum. Regardless of the personality potential he may have inherited, the way any child turns out depends on what happens to him in life, the way you treat him, the way he *interacts* with his environment.

Regardless of what he is born to be, the way he expresses his inborn characteristics will depend heavily on the way his parents treat him. Dr. Chess gives the following examples:

Suppose there are two children, Ralph and Jerry, who both by natural instinct back off quietly from anything new. Ralph's mother respects the fact that her son is slow to warm up, and presents things to him slowly and gently. Gradually he becomes more flexible. Jerry's mother, on the other hand, insists that her son accept the new when and as it is offered. Jerry, in resisting her too-firm demands, becomes even more inflexible.

Or take two babies with violent, explosive tempers. Jane's mother shows inexhaustible patience, meets violence with calm, and tries to keep her child out of difficult situations that would set her off. Gradually, Jane reacts to this calmness and becomes more restrained herself. Tony's mother meets violence with violence, and Tony, as a result, becomes even more explosive.

If one of your own children expresses personality characteristics that tend to give trouble, try thinking of contrasting ways you might treat him, and evaluate their probable results.

So there are these two things to think about: first, what is your child's basic inborn individuality, and, second, how does your own way of treating him affect that individuality?

But there is more to it than that. According to pediatrician T. Berry Brazleton, not only is each child born with a basic potential, and not only is that potential influenced in its expression by the way you treat him, but also the kind of child you have produced will affect *you* and to some extent will determine the kind of parent you can be to him.

Some of you may already have discovered that you are able to do a great job of parenting with one of your children. You feel comfortable with him, you know just what to do with him, and things tend to turn out well for both of you. With him you may feel that you are really a pretty good parent.

With some other child or children it may seem that you can hardly do anything right. Even as babies, some children just rub some mothers the wrong way. You are always at odds. Dr. Brazleton describes this important and exciting notion in his book *Infants and Mothers* (10), which we recommend to all new parents.

A new way of looking at basic personality differences based on inherited physical endowment has recently been offered by pediatrician Lendon H. Smith. In his extremely useful book, *Feed Your Kids Right* (67), he points out to parents that proper nutrition will maintain an individual in health that is optimal for his or her genetic endowment. This book will help parents feed their child or children "properly" in view of the latest information available. Most children, if adequately fed, could be healthier (and thus happier) than they are.

But, Smith points out, children are born with potentially different levels of health ranging from Level One (superb good health) down through Level Four (at which level the child, even though well fed, will need almost constant medical attention). Level Five includes those unfortunate children who may be bedridden, malformed, or extremely retarded.

Thus the level of health which you can anticipate, and which is to quite an extent a part of the child's basic individuality, will nevertheless depend to some extent on the things you feed him. Often the mere elimination of so-called antinutrients (refined sugar, excessive carbohydrates, artificial additives) may be all the help a child needs to raise him from one level of functioning to the next higher level.

Something else that may be interesting is to think about some of your child's personality characteristics in terms of what other members of the family have been like. It can help you respect the genetic or inherited basis of a behavior to see in one of your children some action or way of behaving that you yourself have seen in your own parent or one of your ancestors. It is extremely touching to see in a child of your own things he has unquestionably inherited from earlier ancestors. As Thomas Hardy puts it in his poem "Heredity":

> I am the family face;
> Flesh perishes. I live on,
> Projecting trait and trace
> Through time to times anon,
> And leaping from place to place
> Over oblivion.

Sex Differences

People argue a lot nowadays about whether little boys behave differently from little girls because of their biological differences, or whether we ourselves by our expectations create outstanding differences between the sexes.

Our own personal observations, as well as the literature we have read, indicate that for the most part boys behave in masculine and girls behave in feminine ways because of the way their bodies are structured. Admittedly, society expects certain things of girls and certain other things of boys, but it is our feeling that society came to expect the things it did because of the way people behaved in the first place. It seems probable that if for the most part boys had not behaved boyishly and girls had not behaved girlishly, society would have developed different expectations.

It is generally accepted that boys are physically less strong and resistant to illness in the months after birth and

PLAYING HOUSE

Gesell Institute

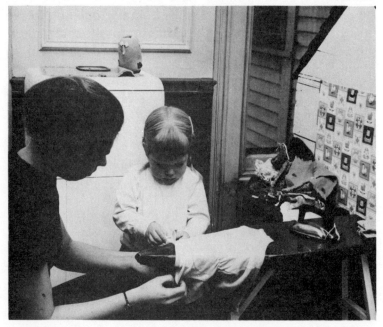

in the childhood years that follow than are girls. As babies and preschoolers, boys tend to be much harder to raise than girls. And boys develop more slowly than girls do in the first twelve or so years of life. They tend to walk later, to talk later, to be toilet trained later.

On the average, boys tend to be some six months slower in their development than girls. Our own most recent comparison of the difference in maturity level between girls and boys (3) indicates that of fifty-nine specific comparisons of the ages at which boys and girls are able to perform successfully on the various Gesell Behavior Tests, girls are more advanced in fifty instances, boys in seven, the two sexes are equally mature on only two tests.

BOY WITH TRUCK

Carol Holt

Ideally, when it comes time for school, boys should start kindergarten and first grade a good six months later than girls do. If they did this, not only would they be more successful in school, but might avoid that awkward time in the early teens when girls are so much more mature than boys in their same school grade, both physically and socially.

However, we do agree with those who hold a point of view quite different from our own that whatever Nature determined, society certainly has supported and nourished the notion that boys should be boyish and girls should be girlish. We definitely go along with those who urge parents to permit the gentler side of their sons to flourish as well as the more forceful side of their daughters' personalities.

Most parents do permit, and even admire, a certain tomboyishness in their daughters. All too many frown on and prohibit any sign of softness in their sons. All too many forcefully push their boys away from quiet, scholarly pursuits and ways of reacting, toward rough, tough, supposedly "manly" ways of being. Do remember that many a little boy, left to his own devices, would not join the Little League.

Even in infancy, it seems that more boy babies, often of a more mesomorphic structure than their sisters, do give an appearance of what we think of as masculinity. Few boy babies react in the coy manner often assumed spontaneously by little girls.

Studies in nursery-school settings reveal that even as early as two years of age, boys tend to be more interested in wheels and cars, girls in dolls. Girls know people's names; boys as a rule do not. Even by three-and-a-half years of age, boys tend to engage in building play. As the school year proceeds, they become more and more interested in imitating grown-up male pursuits, such as being firemen, sailors, and such. Girls play mostly with other girls and prefer such activities as playing house.

At four, boys are wilder than girls. However, they tend to stick longer to some one single type of play. Girls flit from one thing to another. Boys play especially with blocks, cars, and trucks while girls continue with more people-oriented play.

And there is no question that the four-year-old boys, all untutored, do swagger around in what they consider a real tough manner, talking out of the sides of their mouths and calling each other what they consider to be strong masculine names—Bill, John, Mike (usually not their real names).

At the same time, boys very often spontaneously make for the doll corner, or the costume box, and the costumes they choose for themselves often run to dresses and scarves. In deference to the many small boys who would *like* to and are not permitted to have a doll of their own we quote at some length from a charming child's story— *William's Doll,* by Charlotte Zolotow.

William wanted a doll.
He wanted to hug it
and cradle it in his arms
and give it a bottle
and take it to the park
and push it in the swing
and bring it back home
and undress it
and put it to bed
and pull down the shades
and kiss it goodnight
and watch its eyes close
and then
William wanted to wake it
   up
in the morning
when the sun came in

and start all over again
just as though he were its
   father
and it were his child.
"A doll!" said his brother.
"Don't be a creep!"
"Sissy, sissy, sissy!" said the
   boy next door.
"How would you like a
   basketball?" his father
   said.
But William wanted a doll.
It would have blue eyes
and curly eyelashes
and a long white dress
and a bonnet
and when the eyes closed

they would make a little click
like the doll that belonged
to Nancy next door.
"Creepy" said his brother.
"Sissy sissy" chanted the boy
    next door.
And his father brought home
a smooth round basketball
and climbed up a ladder
and attached a net to the ga-
    rage
and showed William
how to jump as he threw the
    ball
so that it went
through the net
and bounced down
into his arms again.
He practiced a lot
and got good at it
but it had nothing to do
with the doll.
William still wanted one.
One day
his grandmother came to
    visit.
William showed her
how he could throw the ball
through the net
attached to the garage out-
    side.
She was very interested
and they went for a walk
    together
and William said,
"But you know
what I really want is a doll."
"Wonderful," said his
    grandmother.

"No," William said.
"My brother says
it will make me a creep
and the boy next door
says I'm a sissy
and my father
brings me other things in-
    stead.
"Nonsense," said his
    grandmother.
She went to the store and
chose a baby doll
with curly eyelashes
and a long white dress
and a bonnet.
The doll had blue eyes
and when they closed
they made a clicking sound
and William loved it
right away.
But his father was upset.
"He's a boy!" he said
to William's grandmother.
"He has a basketball
and an electric train
and a workbench
to build things with.
Why does he need a doll?"
William's grandmother
    smiled.
"He needs it," she said,
"to hug
and to cradle
and to take to the park
so that
when he's a father
like you,
he'll know how to
take care of his baby

and feed him
and love him
and bring him
the things he wants,

like a doll
so that he can
practice being
a father."

And for those mothers who wish their daughters to grow up uninhibited by the usual feminine stereotypes we suggest *Girls Can Be Anything* by Norma Klein, the story of a little girl who didn't want to play nurse, but wanted to play doctor, didn't want to be a stewardess, but wanted to be the pilot, didn't want to be the President's wife, but wanted to be President. Her boy playmate at first objects, but finally they decide to more or less take turns and things work out fine.

Much current emphasis is given to the development of the young child's sense of self, his sense of identity or of individuality. A strong aid to the child's awareness of his own sense of self can be his parents' first understanding him for what he is.

Parents who have more than one child always tend to be struck by the uniqueness of each individual. To be aware of your child's individuality and then to give him the opportunity of expressing and finally understanding that individuality are among the most important things you can do for him.

5/
What You CAN Do:
Know Infancy

"If only we could throw away our first child and start all over again with the second. We made so many mistakes on the first one." This is a common and presumably humorous remark made by young parents, and it would make one feel that perhaps a first baby is handicapped indeed.

Fortunately there is much to balance a parent's inexperience. And that is that the first baby *does* come first and for that very reason is probably more admired and noticed than any child who may come after. His first smile, first word, first step are probably more waited for and appreciated than is anything that younger brothers or sisters might do.

It seems reasonable that the special attention and the privilege and security of being, at least for a time, the only one, may more than make up for the fact that every first child is, admittedly, being raised by inexperienced parents.

Whether the baby you are enjoying and observing is your first or last, infancy does come first, and it teaches the observant parent many interesting and important lessons. Your baby has much, in fact almost everything, to learn and you can learn right along with him.

Perhaps the most important things you have to learn are these two. First, you will note that even the simplest and most basic behaviors develop through a predictable series of patterned stages. And, second, you will find that you cannot do very much to hasten these stages.

Consider one of the most basic behaviors of all, locomotion. You will see, if you observe very carefully, that your baby goes through many preliminary stages before he can walk. First of all, he must lift his head from the flat surface on which he lies. Then he will thrust one knee forward beside his body.

A little later he pivots in a circular direction, and later still he pulls his weight forward over his forearms, dragging body and legs, in what we call a crawling move. Then finally comes that glorious day—he is somewhere around nine or ten months of age—when he manages to push his legs forward and under his body and to lift his abdomen up off the floor. Shortly thereafter he will creep.

All or nearly all of this has to take place before he is going to be ready to walk. (Admittedly some very extensor children do skip the crawling or the creeping stages.) Most parents realize that their baby will in all likelihood need to creep before he can walk. Most do not try, very rigorously or anxiously, to hurry along either creeping or walking. Most are calm if their baby creeps a little later, walks a little later, than some other baby in the family or neighborhood.

Almost everybody realizes that though you may encourage and applaud, you do not need to *teach* your baby either to creep or to walk. The same rule holds true, as all parents know, for that other important and basic behavior —talking. Babies make little sounds before they say real words, speak with single words before they say sentences. Certainly language can be encouraged by your talking to your baby and showing appreciation of his sounds and syllables. But you do not, and do not need to, *teach* him to talk.

Other behaviors, too, develop in their own natural, uncoached sequences. At first your baby reaches for objects so awkwardly that he may actually knock them farther away from him than they were to start with. Gradually he manages to get hold of them, in a crude, pawlike grasp. Soon, without your telling him what to do or teaching him, his grasp becomes so refined that even before one year of age he is picking up tiny objects with an admirably precise grasp between thumb and forefinger.

These behaviors, you will observe, are programmed into him, and they develop with you doing little more than putting him on a flat surface, or providing him with somebody to talk to or an object to grasp. You do not have to *teach* a baby to creep, talk or handle objects. You don't have to teach him to walk, even though you may give natural encouragement and applause.

In fact, if you think about it, you don't have to do too much more about some of the basic behaviors than you do about his teething. Much of a child's behavior, like much about his body, grows in a patterned, predictable, and remarkably spontaneous way. *It is not all up to you.*

This often comes as rather a big surprise to the eager, earnest, conscientious parent of a first baby, but think how much you can be spared by knowing it.

Think, if you will for a minute, how hard it would be if your baby had no instinctive notion of what it was like to creep and walk, or to talk; how difficult it would be if you had to *teach* it all to him. Fortunately you don't have to and you know it, or at least you soon find it out.

Can you believe, and will you accept the fact that many, many of the other things he will need to know and to do will develop just as easily, just as naturally? You provide the background, opportunity, encouragement. Nature will take care of much of the rest.

You do, admittedly, have to provide a few necessary assistances and props. It would be difficult indeed for a child to creep unless he had a more or less stable surface on which to maneuver. Possibly many children would not talk if there were nobody talking to them or for them to talk to. Your encouragement and applause not only stimulate the child but motivate him to the point that he will repeat an applauded behavior.

Most of the other things beyond simple walking, talking, reaching and grasping will be accomplished with equal ease and naturalness and with little more than encouragement, and possibly example and reward, from you.

With aging, admittedly, life becomes more complex. Creeping requires only a stable surface on which to creep and a body which has reached a certain level of maturity. Talking for the most part requires another person to talk to. Later, more complex behaviors require even more props. Reading, quite obviously, requires a book or other printed matter from which to read. Writing requires paper and pencil, pen, crayon or other writing material. And so it goes. As the child matures, the behavior in question, whatever it may be, requires an increasing amount of equipment, opportunity, or other people involved. But the message remains the same: *It is not all up to you.*

It is difficult for us to imagine that many mothers need specific advice about how to play with their children. However, it may be that the many mothers we have come in contact with over the years have been supergifted. Thus, if you do need, or would like to have, highly specific advice about what to do with and for your baby, there are plenty of books that provide such advice. Typical is Genevieve Painter's *Teach Your Baby* (55). This highly detailed book gives, for various ages, recommendations like the following:

> Stimulate feeling. While the baby lies on his back, move his arms over his head.
> Stimulate hearing. Tie a little bell on each bootie. He will hear the sound.

Visit friends with baby.
Give him a clean spoon to put in his mouth.
Attach a balloon to his wrist so he can watch it.
Help him play with his feet.
Place a floating toy in the bath water.
Let him feed himself a bit of food with his fingers.
In the bath, if he splashes water on his face, make a
    game of it by laughing.
Let him watch Daddy as he shaves.
Let him feel the bricks of the sidewalk.

However, perhaps the majority of you will find that most of the things that need to be accomplished or achieved by your infant or preschool child will be managed effectively and with only minimal help from you until that fateful day when he begins his formal schooling.

And even here, assuming that he has at least an average intelligence and needed maturity, and normal and reasonable help from the school in the way of the customary teaching and materials, he should be able to do what he needs to do quite easily, naturally, effectively, and comfortably. (Unless, of course, reading and writing are required before he is ready to begin reading and writing.) Around the time of school beginning, even six months can make the difference between ease and success, and failure.

You do not need to *teach* walking and talking and grasping, but can you even hurry them along? Research carried out by Dr. Gesell at the (then) Yale Clinic of Child Development many years ago, indicates that you cannot, even with vast effort, substantially speed up the appearance and development of the basic human behaviors.

Using the now famous co-twin control method of investigation, one of a pair of identical twins was trained in the behavior in question, for instance, stair climbing or talking, while the other was kept in an entirely non-stair or non-language environment. Then, at the end of a given period of time, the non-trained twin was given a chance to climb stairs, or to respond to conversation. In every instance, after only the briefest experience with stairs or language the non-trained twin functioned exactly as well as the twin who had been given the early and intensive training.

The conclusion reached from these experiments was that a very small amount of training or experience with a given stimulus at a later age, when the child was fully ready to express the behavior in question, more than equaled in effectiveness much earnest training given early and before the organism was ready spontaneously to express that behavior.

Two examples from among the many co-twin experiments conducted by Dr. Gesell and his staff will illustrate what co-twin research has to say.

One of our most striking experiments measured the effectiveness of early training in stair climbing. Every morning for six days a week, over a six-week period, beginning when she was forty-six weeks old, Twin T (the trained twin) was given definite stimulation and guidance in climbing a four-tread staircase. (At this time, neither twin had ever climbed stairs.) An attempt was made to entice her to climb the stairs as many times as possible. Each training period lasted for ten minutes.

During the entire period while Twin T was given daily training in stair climbing, Twin C (control twin) was kept in an environment where no stairs were available. When the twins were fifty-three weeks old, and after Twin T had had daily training in stair climbing for six weeks, Twin C was introduced to the stairs.

On the first day, when she was placed at the foot of the four-step staircase, she climbed equally well, equally fast

(13.8 seconds for T, 13.9 seconds for C) and with the same hand/knee pattern as her sister, though she had not been trained or even exposed to stairs at all.

A similar experiment was made with regard to the twins' language behavior, when both girls were nineteen months of age. This experiment was conducted with rigid experimental control. The experimenter and nurse-assistant lived in isolation with the twins, who were temporarily separated from each other. Twin T was given intensive vocabulary training for a period of five weeks, beginning at her eighty-fourth week and continuing through her eighty-ninth week.

During this time, Twin C was isolated from Twin T and from all other persons except the nurse and the experimenter. These two refrained from talking in C's presence, but communicated with her by gestures, the experimenter using smiling, humming, wordless singing and dramatic game play.

At the close of Twin T's five-week training period, Twin C, then eighty-nine weeks old, was trained for a period of four weeks. Her training was as nearly identical with that given to Twin T (earlier) as was possible. C was consistently ahead of T when a comparison was made on the basis of days of training. In other words, C learned more rapidly than T who had been five weeks younger when she was trained.

Once again, it was clearly demonstrated that learning, even in a highly socialized function such as speech, does not transcend even slight differences in maturity. The environment, important as it is, appears to be strictly limited in what it can teach a child to do. Added age appears to do more in helping any child to learn and express a given behavior than does even quite intensive training at a too-early age.

Special Cribs and Toys

Now comes a question that many mothers and fathers ask. How essential to a baby's intellectual welfare are the elaborate infant cribs briefly offered, and the many very special and expensive toys for infants now on the market? Does your baby really need them? Will their availability actually increase or improve his or her intellectual functioning?

Our reply would be that they are not really needed and that so far as is known they will not increase intelligence.

The most extreme example of the hard sell was the claim made by some manufacturers of the elaborate infant cribs offered by manufacturers in the mid 1970's that your baby would be greatly deprived if you just let him lie there in an old-fashioned crib with only the ordinary and usual things to look at or play with.

We all agree, specialists and experienced parents alike, that a young baby should not be just left lying, always in one position, with nothing to play with, in a crib that is placed in such a way that he has little to look at. On the other hand, we and apparently many others were more than a little skeptical about the need of a "sight line with transparent plastic snap-on pockets hung across the crib, with new family photos, objects, shapes, and textures provided in the pockets; or of a tough, transparent vinyl pouch filled with water and live fish hung on the side of the crib."

Certainly there are many things you can provide for your baby to handle or look at. Mobiles are fun, especially if they are hung on flexible elastic so that the baby can, if he likes, pull them toward him. But even here care should be exercised. Parents who have eagerly hung up these little mobiles in the earliest weeks when admittedly a baby can look but is too young to reach, have found to their dismay that this too early stimulation of vision may have done more harm than good. Early enough around sixteen weeks of age or even a little later.

Just don't push. Don't think too much about your baby's intellectual development. Better in infancy to provide those interesting toys and other stimuli a little too late and casually, than a little too early and overeagerly.

We do, of course, believe in reasonable stimulation. But most psychologists who talk about "infant stimulation" are referring to something more than the provision of ordinary toys and objects. They refer to very special toys and very special teaching and training. They would even "teach" a baby to clap its hands, or even more ridiculous, to learn arithmetic.

Anyone who has ever watched the behavior of a normal infant will appreciate that the very simplest toy or household object, in fact even his own hands or a leaf or a ray of sunshine, can keep him happily busy. Just lying on his back in his crib, or sitting upright, the ordinary baby tends to be busy every minute of his waking life.

One of the most prominent instincts and drives of any infant is his strong drive to move from one place to another. Since, when very young, he cannot walk, and since locomotion when lying on one's back is impractical for most, the normal thing for most babies is to creep and crawl. Most infants do these things as normally and easily as fish swim.

Yet even here the toy manufacturers intrude with an object called Hipp-Along, a flat little thing with casters, which, the ads tell us, is "an ideal pal for the child just beginning to creep." To our way of thinking, your baby can do without this pal.

Another prominent drive in infancy is the drive to reach and grasp. Very early indeed the baby likes to look at his own hand, and by thirty-six weeks he can spend enthralled moments, enchanted by the fact that he can rotate his wrist. A forty-week infant enjoys the fact that he can free his forefinger from his other fingers and thus poke at a little block. If a second block is added, he will vastly enjoy grasping one in each hand and combining the two. These blocks do not have to be fancy.

A year-old infant enjoys little more than dropping something to the floor as he sits in his highchair and having you return it to him so that he can drop it again.

Behavior develops slowly. Each new simple ability delights a growing baby. It does not require a vast amount of technology or a large expenditure of money to provide your growing infant with all that he needs. It does, however, take time on your part. It does take interest. It does take love.

Once today's infant graduates from his excitable crib with its abundant variety of sights and sounds, he is not to be left without stimulation. Right through the preschool years, elaborate mechanical toys are offered. Dolls walk, talk, eliminate. Mothers and fathers have noted, and many have regretted, that typewriters, telephones, cash registers, and computers as well as other mechanical objects, have been scaled down so that toddlers can play with these inappropriate adult devices.

As Elizabeth Harlan, mother of a two-year-old, comments in a recent issue of *Harper's* magazine:

Robbed of wonder and delight, we have set about producing in replica scale models of ourselves and all the things of our existence for our children to play with.

My child grows and changes every day and year, yet I still remember that he once believed his tiny hands might grasp the wind. The wheel and lever must be wonderful to discover. Soap bubbles can still be blown through finger circles in the bath (cost free). Clouds have never ceased to take the form of what we see. The wind and rain have not yet been packaged in styrofoam, and the sun and stars were not put out by Fisher-Price in plastic this year.

The toys that are best for our infants and young children can be, and perhaps ideally should be, extremely simple, inexpensive, and unselfconscious. The very best toys are the ones that are fun to play with. If they also teach something or other, fine, but the ideal toys for children are only indirectly educational.

Infant Norms

Though we obviously are not much in sympathy with strenuous parental efforts to make babies smarter or quicker than they might naturally be, we do sympathize with mothers and fathers who would like to know how their own special baby is doing compared with other babies of his age.

Hopefully, most readers will recognize that individual differences in the rate of development are tremendous. A normal baby might walk as early as ten or eleven months, while another just as normal might not walk till sixteen or even eighteen months. Some little girls talk very early; some little boys, very late.

But because many parents do like to know what to expect of their babies and when to expect it, we list here a few of the more basic infant behaviors and indicate when, *on the average,* one may expect them. We provide these items with an important warning about norms.

Norms, as presumably most of you know, are no more than averages. When one says that at a certain age the norm is for an infant or child to do so and so, the fact that the behavior described is merely an average means that as many will do the thing later as will do it earlier.

A series of norms thus tells you the *order* in which you can expect behaviors to occur and when on the average they will occur. They do *not* tell you when the behavior *will* occur in your own infant or child or even when it *should* occur. They merely give you a clue to how things go in general.

If checking your own child's behavior with such norms is interesting to you, here are a few things that, on the average, we may expect babies to do in the first year of life. Remember, though, that *you are not to worry* if your own baby is a little slower in some things than these averages suggest.

Four weeks:

> Lying on his back, your baby will probably extend the arm on the side that he faces and will flex the other arm (tonic neck reflex).
> He will probably be able to roll partway to one side.
> Placed on his stomach, he will be able to lift his head slightly.
> He looks at things directly in his line of vision.
> He does not reach for objects, but his fingers will close on things placed directly in the palm of his hand.
> Vocalization doesn't go much beyond small, throaty sounds, and many do not smile until as late as six weeks of age.

Sixteen weeks:

> As the baby lies on his back, arm posture is more symmetric (even), and he will grasp an object presented overhead.
> He also enjoys fingering his own fingers.
> Placed on his stomach, he is almost able to roll to his back. He lifts head rather high and may at the same time lift his legs, so that weight is on abdomen only.
> He can sit up if given much support. Likes to look at his own hands.
> All now smile and laugh and can "say" little syllables such as "ah-uh-eh." Also coo, gurgle, and blow bubbles.
> Baby now "knows" his mother, turns his head at the sound of a voice, still "accepts" strangers though he will not do so later on, as he becomes more aware of differences in people.

Twenty-eight weeks:

There is now much that he can do.

He no longer is content to spend long periods lying on his back, preferring to sit, or to lie on his stomach.

Many can sit momentarily, leaning forward on their own hands.

If held upright, baby will take much of his own weight and may bounce when held standing.

Is not quite ready yet to crawl but may move somewhat in a circular direction.

He now likes to hold things in his hands, though his grasp is still crude and pawlike.

Many are beginning to make an "mm" sound but not a real word.

Now may be quite responsive to social advances from others.

Is now mature enough to enjoy looking at himself in a mirror and may even pat the glass.

Lying on his back he is very agile and may easily get his feet to his mouth.

Most now take solids well.

Forty weeks:

The baby now has come a long way. He is no longer interested in lying on his back, and can sit with ease and no support.

Placed on his stomach, he can usually get up to his knees and may creep. Placed in his playpen, he is very likely to pull himself to his feet. He is extremely agile.

Now he loves to handle objects, and his grasp has become increasingly delicate. He may even poke at things with an extended forefinger.

He can bring two blocks (one held in each hand) together in front of him.

He now tends to be extremely social with other people or with his mirror image, which he pats, smiles at, talks to.

And, wonder of wonders, he now talks, saying such important words as "Da-da" or "Mum-mum."

He responds to "bye-bye" and may be ready for pat-a-cake.

He may already have his own favorite toys.

Many are now shy with strangers.

Fifty-two weeks:

And now your baby may very likely be so skillful in the upright position that he may be able to take a few steps, alongside furniture or if you hold his hand.

On his stomach he tends to creep with great agility and speed.

He may no longer be content to remain in his playpen for more than short periods.

He is now extremely skillful in handling even very small objects, holding them between thumb and forefinger.

Sitting in highchair, he likes to drop things on the floor and then have you give them back to him.

He will, as a rule, give you things if you ask him, or will respond to a very simple command.

He may inhibit a forbidden action if you say "no no."

May love pat-a-cake and peek-a-boo.

He may still be shy with strangers.

Many now have two or three words besides "Da-da" and "Mum-mum."

Enjoys his toys, enjoys moving about, enjoys social interchange with other persons.

He may now co-operate a little as you dress him.

So, infancy comes first and it teaches many lessons. These lessons are fairly easy to learn for many, because they appear so clearly. As our children grow older, we sometimes lose track of reality by confusing what actually happens with what we would like to have happen. But when they are still infants, as a rule, our feelings about the way they ought to be doing things have really not yet gotten into high gear. Most people can look at their babies, if not objectively, at least with much greater relaxation and clarity than they will manage later on.

Thus, even if you think your baby is unusually bright, you do not as a rule feel that because of that brightness he should be able to do things any earlier than he actually does do them. This, perhaps, is the first lesson that infancy teaches us: it is a good idea to view any child's behavior and abilities objectively, without getting them mixed up with your own hopes and plans or your estimate of his intelligence.

Second, you will soon appreciate, as you watch your baby develop, that most of the important things he needs to do he will do by himself, with only a minimum of teaching or help from you. Most parents learn very soon, as they watch their babies, that they cannot, even with considerable effort, substantially speed up the various stages of behavior. Also you will find that it does not require elaborate or expensive toys to keep your baby happy.

Next, though many of you will undoubtedly try to make your child more athletic, or more bookish, or more sociable than Nature probably had in mind, most of you do accept his basic individuality as it expresses itself in infancy, fairly calmly: "She's so stolid"; "He's never still"; "He's always smiling"; "The least thing upsets her."

Those of you who from good luck, good judgment, or a good generous feeling about individual differences, or because you have a good pediatrician, have permitted your baby a self-demand and self-regulation feeding and sleeping schedule will have learned something special, and something that is important. This is that every child, from the time he is born (even some say from before he is born) is an individual. Watch your baby as he expresses his feeding needs. Even here he tells you a good deal about his basic personality.

Some babies seem to know exactly when and how much they want to eat (or drink). They approach their feeding time with eagerness, nurse enthusiastically, know when they are finished, and then settle down to sleep.

Others do not seem to know whether they want a feeding or not, suck intermittently, seem to be finished and then want more. Some seem to need a feeding every three hours; others can easily wait for four. Some give up their middle-of-the-night feeding very early; others cling to it.

Some flourish and gain weight easily. Others are colicky, cranky, and need many tries before you can find a formula that suits them. In fact, the wants of some babies seem so ill-defined that it may be too difficult to set up a self-demand schedule with them. Such babies need to have their mother impose a schedule, making up their minds for them, as it were.

The other half of self-demand, one that some mothers and some babies overlook, is *self-regulation,* that is, in providing a self-demand schedule, a mother at first fits her schedule to the baby's demand. But before many weeks she expects him to show increasing self-control and to make his own adaptations so that before long a schedule is arrived at which is convenient for *both* mother and baby. Some babies are great at the self-demand part of this arrangement, but less good at the part where they, too, are expected to adapt.

Many, many other facets of your child's basic personality will be clear to you by the end of his first year. Yours may be a baby who develops evenly and predictably. Or he may be a "spurt and plateau" baby, one who for long periods does not seem to progress at all but stays, seemingly forever, on some plateau, and then suddenly leaps forward to some new level of maturity.

Or he may be one who makes recurring big advances, often more than he can maintain, so that it is as if he advances two steps and then falls back one.

There are babies who love the new adventure and others who cling to the old and hate anything new. There are those who seemingly can adjust to anything and others who need great help in making even the smallest adaptation.

There are those who love people and who seem happiest in company; others who accept very few outside the immediate family and seem perfectly content to be alone. Some babies can entertain themselves for minutes if not hours at a time. Others demand almost constant attention.

These and many, many other important individual differences make themselves evident in babies almost from the beginning. If you do your homework and learn the lesson of your own child's personality during his infancy, it will make his childhood easier and more satisfactory for him as well as for you.

6
What You CAN Do: Keep Your Child Healthy and Well Nourished

One of the most important things that any parent can do for a child is to make every possible effort to feed him right and to keep him in optimal health.

Up till just a few years ago the conscientious parent interested in his or her child's nutrition concentrated on providing foods from each of the four basic food groups: fruits and vegetables, milk and dairy products, meat and other sources of protein, and cereal grains. There was also a general feeling that "too many sweets" were bad for a child. But the level of public sophistication about nutrition was low.

Then in 1975 a highly controversial book by Dr. Ben Feingold of California—*Why Your Child Is Hyperactive* (26)—appeared. Dr. Feingold suggested that millions of children in this country who suffer from hyperkinesis (overactivity) and resulting learning difficulties, can be helped dramatically by removing all food additives and artificial coloring and flavoring from their diets.

This seemingly simple concept inspired a concern about diet which went far beyond Dr. Feingold's original proposition. All over the country so-called Feingold parent groups sprang up, and it now seems to be established beyond doubt that the removal of artificial food flavorings and colorings from a child's diet can in many instances substantially calm down and thus improve the behavior of the hyperactive child.

A next step which amounts to a revolution in our way of looking at nutrition was taken by Oregon pediatrician Lendon H. Smith in his book titled *Improving Your Child's Behavior Chemistry* (66). According to Dr. Smith, many children turn out badly in school and in life because their bodies do not work right. The cause of this poor functioning is often an improper diet, especially the ingestion of too much white flour and sugar. Eating too much sugar produces a rapid rise in blood sugar. Usually the body responds by producing insulin, causing the blood sugar level to fall. The child then experiences wide mood swings and marked changes in his energy level. This results in behavior which may be unpredictable at best; violent at worst. The Dr. Jekyl/Mr. Hyde child who is so good one minute and so out-of-control, irritable or violent the next may actually be suffering from this kind of condition, due to improper diet.

Dr. Smith has now taken a further step which can be helpful to parents. In his 1979 book *Feed Your Kids Right* (67) he gives very specific dietary suggestions. He points out that even with the best will in the world we may fail in our efforts to feed our children right if we include in their diet too many "antinutrients."

An antinutrient is a substance which when consumed not only fails to provide nourishment but increases the body's need for more nutrients such as vitamins. Among the antinutrients which Dr. Smith feels should in general be avoided are sugar, commercial ice cream, boxed cereals, white flour, and homogenized pasteurized milk. If a food has been packaged, processed, added to, stablized, emulsified, colored or preserved, you know it is out of Nature's hands.

Since many antinutrients tend, as mentioned above, to cause a lowering of blood sugar in the body, they can result in antisocial or depressed behavior. They can also, in some cases, bring on a wide variety of physical symptoms, from allergies to arthritis.

Thus a parent's best bet is to do his or her best to omit antinutrients from a child's diet and to see to it that he or she eats natural foods in frequent, small amounts. Good, natural foods include raw vegetables, white cheese, nuts, fish, chicken, peas and beans, raw fruits. Often this combination of the removal of antinutrients and their replacement with wholesome foods can be enough to raise a child to a whole new level of good health.

Also, though this as well as any major change in diet will best be carried out under the direction of your own physician, you may wish to have your child begin a daily intake of vitamins or minerals. And since we are all different from each other, it is important to find each child's own specific requirement, not just for survival (which is the value of the government's Recommended Daily Allowance—RDA) but for optimal health. Dr. Smith provides safe and sensible guidelines in *Feed Your Kids Right* (67).

Most of these suggestions about nutrition apply rather generally to most any boy or girl. However, since each child is in many ways different from every other, it is quite possible that any child may actually be allergic to some or many ordinary food products. If your child is overactive, never still, unable to concentrate, suffers from chronic fatigue, has dark circles under his eyes or suffers from a more or less constant stuffy nose, Dr. William Crook of Tennessee suggests that a parent might attempt on his or her own to discover the cause.

He suggests that you might try a so-called elimination diet. In brief, in your effort to discover what if any foods your child is allergic to, you eliminate his favorite foods for a week or so. The main foods which are likely to cause trouble include milk and all dairy products, egg, wheat, corn, sugar, oranges and other citrus fruit, chocolate, and food coloring, flavoring and preservatives. If your child does have a food allergy, the removal of these foods should cause his symptoms to disappear.

After a week or so you then return the foods, one at a time and only one on any given day. If adverse symptoms return, you will have a good idea of what food is causing the child's difficulties.

Any attempt such as this might best be carried out under the supervision of your own physician. But you can get a good idea of what would be involved by reading Dr. Crook's book titled *Tracking Down Hidden Food Allergy* (18).

A last consideration: children like adults can be allergic not only to foods but also to any other aspect of the environment—including grasses, trees, dust, molds, odors. People have been aware of the problem of allergies for many years now—but current knowledge is becoming increasingly sophisticated.

If your child's body or behavior do seem to you to be under par, you might be well advised to seek the help of a physician who is knowledgeable about both nutrition and allergies. A relatively small bit of help can often make a very big difference in a child's general health.

Whenever health problems arise, if a good checkup from a reliable internist reveals no infection, no surgical condition, you might be wise to seek out a physician who is nutrition-minded. So-called orthomolecular* doctors practice on the theory that if all the cells of the body are properly nourished, the body should be able to withstand even a rather hostile environment—stress including infections, injuries, emotional trauma, and the normal wear

---

*A term coined by Linus Pauling to mean the right nutrients in the right amounts. The idea is to correct any biochemical imbalance by using substances that are native to the body, such as wholesome foods and vitamin and mineral supplements.

and tear experienced by a growing youngster. Fortunately biochemistry has now reached the point where all the important chemicals needed by the body, and present in foods, are probably known.

You and your children can be healthier than most people are. The knowledge is available. It's up to you to find it and use it.

7 /
What You CAN Do: Help Your Child to Know Himself

There are many things you can do with and for your child that will provide the "optimum growing conditions" designed to assure that he will develop to his fullest potential. All these things are designed to help him learn about himself, about the world around him and how he can use his skills and abilities to interact most effectively with that world. As you will see, most of the things that we recommend for you to do with your preschooler will be very natural to many of you.

What you may not have realized is that these easy things you do quite naturally will benefit your child. There is purpose in the seemingly simple activities that the two of you share. It is easy to provide activities and a setting in which your child can be assured of getting maximum feedback, especially that special, personal feedback you yourself give in attending to and reacting to him and to the things he does.

Spend time with your child: Perhaps the most important thing you can do is spend time with your child. Remember, it is not time spent in the same house or even in the same room with him that counts. What counts is the time that is spent really being with him, talking to him, laughing with him, playing with him. Listen if he wants to tell you something. Look if he wants to show you something. Make him realize that he is important to you and that the things which interest him also interest you. Some parents find it helpful to establish a special time they call their "children's hour"—a time set aside to do things with the child, time shared with no other person or activity.

Enjoy your child: We are told that one thing which distinguishes the American culture from some others of the world is our unfortunate failure to enjoy our children. Enjoyment is not something that can be faked, but enjoyment can be learned. And though it comes easily to some parents, many do have to *learn* to enjoy their children. Some of us have been trapped with the "shoulds" of society, which say that in order for us to be happy with our children, the children must first be behaving "properly." We get so tied up with worrying about whether our children are being "good" that we sometimes forget to enjoy them.

One prerequisite to enjoying children is to provide a setting for them in which their natural behaviors are not judged as good or bad but are, for the most part, accepted. Nursery school provides one such setting, but the home could, with thought, provide another.

We need places where we can relax with children, be alive with them, learn with them, see things again as for the first time, places where they are not held down by adult expectancies. Take a child to a museum that does not permit touching, and you have defeated your purpose. Try taking him, instead, to a place where he can look and touch and explore, where you can enjoy just being with him as well as experience the pleasure of watching him discover.

Let your child enjoy himself: There was a time, not too long ago, when the major concern of many parents was the child's deportment. They wanted him to be "good," to behave "nicely," to be a credit to the family. Most parents still want their children to behave well, but this is no longer necessarily their prime concern.

Then came a time when American parents became overenthusiastic about the actually very solid and interesting things the Swiss psychologist Jean Piaget had to say about the way that thinking develops. Some became excessively interested in the so-called cognitive development of their children. This is a reasonable kind of interest, though we shall attempt to convince you that most of you do not need to be actively or anxiously concerned about your children's thinking.

Today, though these first two aspects of behavior remain important, many parents are becoming increasingly concerned about the child's *sense of self*—in how he feels about himself. Many now feel that it is more important for a child to be comfortable and happy with himself as a person than to be entirely well behaved or to excel intellectually.

Dr. Phyllis Harrison-Ross and Barbara Wyden, in their lively book, *The Black Child: A Parent's Guide* (36), give excellent suggestions about things a parent can do to help support and strengthen a child's sense of self. A real-life example of the importance of the sense of self is given in their story of Crystal, a little girl who disliked being black because her mother did not value her own color and had taught Crystal that it wasn't good to be black.

As these authors point out:

This is just about the most crippling thing a parent can do to a child: taking away part of her identity. If Crystal didn't want to be black (and she obviously couldn't be white or yellow or anything else), who and what would she be? She would always be lacking one of the very important elements that make for a healthy self-respect and strong self-image.

Crystal's mother was given assistance in helping Crystal to appreciate that her skin color was a reality. She had to accept and live with it just as she accepted the fact that she had a cute little button nose. It was part of her identity. If she didn't like it, she didn't like part of herself.

That her mother's efforts were successful was demonstrated at a nursery-school open house. In showing her father some sandbox cakes that she had made, Crystal told him, "I used to make white cakes but now I make chocolate cakes. I like them better."

You have a great deal to do with how your child comes to feel and think about himself. The words you use to describe him to himself and to others are words of magic influence. Is he a "clumsy" child, a "thoughtful" child, one who "breaks everything he gets his hands on," "selfish," or "aggressive" or "shy"? Or do you describe him as "happy," "sturdy," "friendly," "capable"? What you say about him is an important part of how he thinks about himself.

If you are overeager, you run the risk of pushing him into things that are difficult for him and beyond his maturity level, and in doing so you set him up for failure. He learns "I can't do it," "My parents aren't pleased with me as I am," "I never make it," "I am a failure." If more restrained, you can see that the tasks required of him are within his current ability level and that they stretch him just enough for him to experience the exhilaration of success. Then he will learn "I can do it," "My parents are pleased with me," "I am a success."

These are the two major ways in which you work to help your child develop a viable self-concept: provide him with accurate but positively oriented feedback from the most important people in the world—his parents—and see that the experiences he has with the rest of the world are geared to provide as much realistic positive feedback as possible.

In helping your child develop a strong sense of self you can program your play with him to take advantage of his currently developed abilities, increasing the complexity of the exercise task with his age. You can play pat-a-cake with him at forty weeks and imitate his movements and crawl and creep with him as he learns to get about. (You will be the sveltest mother on the block.)

When he is two, he can show you his eyes and point to his nose. Later, he will move with you, touching toes, nodding head, closing eyes, and playing guessing games as "I see with my—," "I walk with my—," "I sing with my —," and then act out what he has verbalized. By the time he is four, you will both enjoy modifying these games with jokes: "Stamp with your hands," "Wiggle your eyes," "Close your nose."

Exercise and touching games set to music are fun. Use some of the good old favorites, make up your own, or take advantage of the commercial records for children. Some that you probably know or can learn easily are: "Bend and Stretch," "Put Your Finger in the Air," "Hokey Pokey," "Looby Lou," "Did You Ever See a Lassie?," "Chicken Fat."

Go for a walk: Part of your enjoyment of another person is the way you feel about yourself when you are with him. And as Sparkman and Carmichael point out in *Blueprint for a Brighter Child* (69), you can train yourself to see new beauty in the world about you as you share it with your preschooler. As these authors describe it, a simple walk around the block can be the source of interest and entertainment for you both. In their words:

While we walk slowly along, our child skips and runs and jumps and comes back to greet us with an occasional superficial observation—which presents a wonderful opportunity for enlarged observation. We might stop on the grassy strip by the sidewalk and stoop to examine the blades of grass. Look at the different kinds of grass—the shape of the blades, the color, and the veins running through each blade.

Hours could easily be spent looking for animals living in the grass, perhaps for ants. This would be an excellent time to find pictures of ants in books—especially in children's encylopedias.

What a good way to get a child further interested in books! Now would be a good time to read to him about ants, ant houses, grass, and leaves. You might be interested in buying a glass ant house or in making one of your own.

Did you notice the soil around the ant hill? Is it different from the soil in other places around the block? And how is soil made? Speaking of soil—is soil good or bad? We clean our feet before going inside the house so we won't track soil inside. Does this mean that soil is bad?

Flowers in bloom are a perfect choice to help your child develop the concept of color. *Don't strive to make him memorize the colors around him; merely make him aware of the different colors.* By simply referring to the green grass, the red flower, the black pavement, you will promote color consciousness and color discrimination. Children love games and a good one in this instance is the old-timer, "I see something red. What do I see?" Of course, taking turns is a must.

Look at those trees—see the ways they are alike and the ways they are different? Even the same species are different, yet all have likenesses. There may be a cocoon in one of them—or a bird's nest—or holes where birds have pecked for insects—or knots—or dead limbs. Notice the overall shape of the leaves. Are they round, triangular, pointed?

We haven't looked at the houses yet—the big houses—bigger houses—biggest houses.Which house is smallest? These are important concepts. Or are there clouds in the sky? What do they look like? Can you see faces, animals, buildings, or other figures in the clouds?

For some reason most children get excited about rocks. Rocks are a wonderful source for a collection. Help your child see rocks, feel them—yes, even throw them. See what happens when a rock goes up—when it comes down—when it hits the pavement or ground at an angle—how it sounds—which kinds of rocks break. Count rocks, read about them, look at pictures of them, enjoy their beauty.

We could spend a week on one trip, and if so much can be seen in one block, imagine what marvellous experiences parent and child can have at the zoo, seashore, forest, lake, or wherever they might be. Any place is a place for learning, and if your child has developed a vivid imagination, games and activities can be devised from the most ordinary objects or situations.

See that your child gets plenty of exercise: Every child needs experience in learning to use his body effectively. Movement exploration and exercise provide the child with the physical learning experiences that serve as the basis of much of his living: perception of physical self or body image, sensory awareness, sense of space and direction, appreciation of form. You may well do more for your child's ultimate ability by helping him handle his body effectively than by specifically pushing or concentrating on cognitive development.

As pediatrician Ray Wunderlich (77) has pointed out, admittedly some children are naturally well co-ordinated, and some are awkward. Regardless of natural endowment, any child will benefit from physical exercise, and even the awkward can with practice become better co-ordinated.

Any effort to help your child move comfortably and effectively will be well repaid, since the child with awkward, fragmented movement has to devote excessive energy to the component of movement. On the other hand, the co-ordinated child, moving in a well-oiled automatic smooth pattern, accomplishes his tasks without particular attention to the individual movements involved. Thus his whole energies may be devoted to his task rather than to the movement with which it is to be accomplished.

One necessary basis for learning is a clear knowledge of one's own body and how one can move it effectively, and of where one is in space. One of the first tasks of any infant is to discover which parts of his world are attached to him, which parts he can control. Watch the five-month-old baby—he has learned that his arms are a part of him! But he is still working to understand that his legs belong also. The older child continues this learning task, but now his learning is that of control.

Most children don't need much outside encouragement to exercise, but you can provide extra opportunity for the occasional child who is not a spontaneous mover, and you can reap the added benefit of not only togetherness but added physical control of your own. Take time for exercise yourself every day. And program a way in which your child can participate. Exercises that take two are good for touching each other and enjoying body contact as well as for knowledge of where the body is in space. Some of you, more athletically inclined than others, will enjoy this movement for its own sake; others will exercise as a learning experience for their children.

As Wunderlich (77) emphasizes:

One of the prime needs of children in their growth and development is to know themselves in their own particular setting. It is important for them to know when and how they can change the world and when and how they cannot. Body awareness is strongly involved in this. A thorough, assured knowledge of what one's body can do and what it cannot do, under varied situations, is necessary for confident involvement in life's situations, from infancy onward.

Exercising large muscles: Your preschooler is likely to be so active that you may wonder at the need of providing *more* things for him to use in exercise. We believe that motor learning is a primary task of the preschool years and we encourage you to allow your child all the physical activity possible. If you have no jungle gym in your own yard, find the nearest park or schoolyard, and from the time he is eighteen months old you can give this equipment a good workout. (This is, by the way, a good thing to plan for the teen-age baby-sitter to do with him while you are having your daily break.)

Tricycles are favorite toys from three or earlier and will get good use. Encourage this. And if you live in a place where the child cannot safely play with his trike alone, let him pedal to the park with the sitter, or walk beside him yourself in a sharing time. It is important to pay attention to the energy limit of your own child and not program more physical exercise than he can enjoy without tiring. It will be a long time before he knows his own energy limitations and can stop all by himself before he is too tired. (Some of us never learn.) So your tricycle walk may end at the park, the neighbor's yard, or at the schoolyard, where he can engage in another activity before triking back home.

At home, many of your bending and stretching "body image" exercises will also provide good large-muscle exercise for your child. Don't be shy in serving many purposes with a single type of movement exercise. (Dusting furniture provides good large muscle movement.) Take advantage of seasonal activities, and be aware of how much large-muscle (and body awareness) exercise is involved in putting on the cold-weather apparel even before your

PLAY IN SAND IS FUN AND GOOD EXERCISE

Robert Chase

child gets to tumble and push and build in the snow.

Snow in the winter and, equally so, sand in the summer, are wonderful mediums for promoting all kinds of good exercise as well as fun and relaxation. Seashore, lake, and backyard pool (or, lacking these, just the bathtub) provide wonderful opportunity for large-muscle exercise.

Exercising small muscles: Fine muscle control develops gradually but steadily. You can devise games that encourage exercise of such ability as your child may have developed. Let his interest be your clue in all your planning for him, for if you do not push your preschooler you will find that he will not push himself. He will engage in new activities and new learning as long as it is exciting, interesting, fun, and useful but he will seldom if ever push beyond his capacity to absorb.

Even when the child is two or under, and increasingly thereafter, he will pick up small objects and drop them into a bottle or other object with a small opening. (You must carefully choose relative sizes to insure that he succeeds.) A button box is lots of fun for sorting and provides excellent opportunity for using the small muscles of the hand. Molding and modeling are also good for this. Use clay, play dough, or make your own modeling material with flour. Your child can crumple newspaper and fill a basket, or play with the resultant balls. He can pick up all kinds of things, including clothes and toys. He can squeeze the water out of a sponge or washcloth while he is cleaning the sink or himself.

Improving eye-hand co-ordination: The baby begins to focus his eyes by eight to nine weeks, and from that time forward he uses them, visually perceiving the world around him and judging where his body is in relation to the world he sees. There are many things in the games he plays that are particularly relevant to exercising this ability of knowing where he is and how he is moving in space.

Most ball play is suited to this task, and you can play ball with your child from the time he is very young. You can roll the ball for your infant to follow with his eyes. Later you can roll the ball between you, or he can roll it across the floor and bounce it gently off the wall, or roll it toward a target. Balls may be bounced and caught—with the precaution that if you are going to let the children play ball inside the house, the room should be without fragile objects, or the ball should be of sponge or cotton or plastic. Outside, you will need a fenced space, or an area without traffic.

There are many variations of ball bouncing, each of which is specifically beneficial. Balls can be bounced with the right hand, with the left, or you can alternate by alternating hands. Throw the ball up and catch it on the rebound, clapping hands before catching. Soon you can teach your preschooler the counting or rhyming bouncing-ball games that you knew in elementary school. It is interesting to note that these games are traditionally girls' games—based on the fact that girls do develop at an earlier age the ability to perform at least some of the tasks of these ball games. Actually, boy children, with less ready skill, could well use this kind of exercise. It would seem a good idea to get some of it programmed into your boys as fun things to do before the strong boy-girl identity separation develops.

Children could bat at a light, preschool-size tether ball with their hands.

Pegboard games of all kinds, especially those that allow both copying and free expression, are useful and fun. Be sure that the pegboard you get for the younger child has large pegs and large holes.

Use age-appropriate puzzles from two-and-a-half years up.

Bean bags are fun for throwing and catching.

Or play drop the clothespin into the bottle.

String beads. Again, be sure to choose beads and string

large enough to be comfortably handled by your preschooler. Then he can string at random, or make Mother a necklace of blue (or "all one color," if he has not learned color names), or all one shape, or in a pattern.

Hammering is an activity that allows for the outlet of some frustration as well as providing an excellent eye-hand co-ordination exercise. The pounding boards designed for two-and-a-half-year-olds are used enthusiastically also by much older children. However, for the three-and-a-half- to four-year-old, very soft wood with large nails is highly acceptable from the child's point of view.

Increasing sensory awareness: The child's awareness and sense of self grow as he learns about the many ways in which he can perceive the world. As you have allowed him to experience many things on his walk around the block, you can also help him at home to learn about the smell, sound, sight, taste, and touch of things. Many things around the house can be identified by *smell:* foods in the kitchen, cleaning and soap smells, Daddy's shaving lotion. Make guessing games of identifying the natural odors of his world.

Listen with him. The clock ticks, a car sounds different from a truck going by on the street. There are door bells, and telephone bells, and tricycle bells. Birds sing and crickets chirp. How does a spade sound digging up the garden? Listen to water fall and sand being poured into a pail, a pencil drop from the table.

Taste with him, and at the same time learn more about him. What does he like in the way of tastes? Of consistencies? Carrots and crackers and chocolate are very different to chew. Don't force experimentation but do exploit opportunities when they arise. You may prefer to do this kind of exploring while he is in his highchair, or in a booth at a restaurant, combining the idea of a place to eat with the experience.

Touching, of course, is a great way to develop sensory awareness. Let him feel sand slipping through his fingers and give him lots of water play. Fill the sink with pots and pans to wash. You can fill the tub with soapy water and let him feel his slippery body. He can also wash tables and woodwork, the refrigerator, the shelf. He can wash dolls and doll clothes. Play with mud (probably before his bath). Put different materials, such as sandpaper and velvet, in a bag and let him feel the difference without looking. See how much of his world he can identify by touch alone.

Learning about space and direction: Your child learns about space and direction by climbing up and around and on and through and behind. Make a game of it by setting up obstacle courses—in the living room with the living room furniture, under a table, through a cardboard box, behind a chair. Children can make courses up for themselves and each other. Or Daddy can build a more permanent course in the yard with large drainage pipes, old tires, movable ladders and planks.

Also, every time you ask your child to put a spoon *on* the table, get a carrot *out of* the refrigerator, put the soap *in* the soap dish, put his toy *in* the toy box, you are helping him to learn how things and he himself are positioned in space.

Learning about form: Children learn about form and shape by touching with their bodies and with their eyes. Vision has a great deal to do with the understanding of form. Knowing the names of different shapes, too, is part of coming to a good understanding of form.

There are many things you can do to stimulate your child's interest in and understanding about different forms or shapes. Sturdy building blocks are ideal for giving the child opportunity to learn how shapes look and feel and fit together, combining to make larger wholes. Blocks intrigue the child from earliest preschool through elementary-school years. Clay and other materials for molding and shaping are good for helping the child learn about shape and form, as well.

By two-and-a-half to three years of age, if not before, your child will enjoy toys that allow him to fit three-dimensional cubes and cylinders into holes of the proper shape. Puzzles provide another opportunity to experience the ways in which things fit together.

As soon as your child has learned to identify a new shape, it can be added to the verbal game you play at home, in the car, or anywhere that you find things of different shapes. A rectangle, for instance, can be found in a mirror, the refrigerator, a billboard, or the magazine in the doctor's office. Or you can use books to encourage your child's interest in shapes, as you can to interest him or her in colors, sounds, and numbers, as discussed in the following chapter.

Eyes-closed guessing games about "what shape do you feel" are fun for the older preschooler. Be sure to take *your* turn, letting *him* choose things for *you* to hold and guess.

Nesting toys have always been favorite presents from grandparents. Many grownups remain fascinated by those pretty boxes that open to disclose other, smaller boxes or those larger dolls that contain ever smaller dolls.

As the child's fine muscle development permits (and for exercising these muscles) there are many materials and games which will be interesting and useful. Games that provide many pieces of different shapes for copying and devising patterns are desirable. Mosaic pieces, Leggo, and the perennial Tinker Toy type games are all good choices for establishing a child's sense of form.

Teaching Your Child about Your World and Interests

If you are concerned about *teaching* your child, you will be consciously aware of wanting to reinforce his natural experience with the world. Those things of prime importance to you, the parents, can be emphasized both in your interaction with your child and as you observe him in his environment. If a parent is mathematically oriented, he or she looks at things in terms of their physical relationships. The musically oriented parent notices the sounds and tones in the environment. Thus, with the musically inclined, whenever a bird sings, the song may be mentioned. Musical sounds can be identified by the instrument that makes them. Rhythms can be noted and pointed out. Other parents may be primarily interested in line, in movement, in food, in manners.

You will give your child the vocabulary for differentiation in the area that interests you. You will help him become aware of differences. But, hopefully, you will not push. For instance, don't ask for fine-color differentiation before your child can name colors. Take your cues from what interests him. It is especially important not to scold or show disappointment when he doesn't respond to something you have offered—but be sure to give positive reinforcement when he does respond.

Be aware above all that your attention is the most important reinforcing agent in your child's life. Anything, any behavior that you approve and/or give special attention to will be more likely to occur again. If you like him and like the way he behaves, and show this clearly, you will help him build a reservoir of confidence with which he can approach new situations and new learning, and which will help him to succeed.

8 /
What You CAN Do:
Read to Them

Even the calm and relaxed mother and father, serene and secure in the face of advice that warns it is both your duty and your responsibility to cultivate the preschool mind, may feel that perhaps one ought to be doing *something* intellectual.

If you are thus interested, as many are today, in improving your child's mind, you do not need elaborate equipment, don't need a scholar's understanding of so-called cognitive development, don't need to send your child to a school or center where teachers will self-consciously work to raise his I.Q. and teach him to read.

The best and most important thing you can do for a child, as far as his intellectual development is concerned, is something that many parents have done quite naturally and with great pleasure ever since books were invented. *You read to him.* And when he is getting ready to read for himself, you will know it by two good signs.

First of all, he will look on as you read. Second, he will ask what certain letters, alone or in combination, either in his books or on faucets or packages or street signs spell. Until he does these things of his own accord—and they come late in many children, especially in boys—you might as well save your efforts.

At first your child's interest in books may go no further than a wish to point out, appropriately or inappropriately, the *mummies* and *daddies* and *babies* he sees pictured.

Gradually, he will listen, even though briefly and with much wiggling, to very short stories about everyday affairs. Stories about shoes or about the routine events of a young person's day may be his chief interests.

Reading to a preschooler is not always instantaneously successful. You may need to be flexible in your expectations of success. If, when you first try to read to your child, he wriggles and runs away, don't give up for good. Try again at a different time of day, on a different day, or with a different book.

Or read to another child, or to an adult, or even read aloud to yourself in his presence.

Read to your child because you enjoy it, even if he doesn't. Don't necessarily demand that he sit still and pay full attention. Even if he doesn't listen very well, he may enjoy being with you and having your attention and being cuddled.

One day you may find that he stops his play to look at a picture, but may otherwise play as if he were not listening. One day you will find that even though he has not been able to sit still and attend with his eyes, he has heard the stories, that he has understood something of your own love of books and reading.

Most *do* become interested before very long, and interest span does widen and lengthen. Very few remain permanently uninterested. Increasing enthusiasm for being read to is often accompanied by interest in looking at, if not actually reading, books on their own.

Long before the ordinary child is ready to read, if he is one who enjoys and responds to books, he may go through a stage that at first impresses and delights, later on sometimes irritates and wearies, his parents. Around two-and-a-half to three years of age many children, with the rigidity and compulsiveness characteristic of that age, memorize, or seem to memorize, their storybooks.

At any rate, they KNOW if you skip a word, much less a line. A tired mother, hurrying to get through bedtime rituals, cleverly turns two pages instead of one. Jeremy knows. Or she skips an especially boring paragraph. Teresa remembers. Many, perhaps the brighter ones, tend to insist that books be read line for line and page by page, *exactly* as they were written and exactly as they heard them the very first time around.

For this reason, the truly wise parent, fully aware that strength and patience are limited, selects books that have lots of lovely big pictures and a minimum of text. It is not the amount of type in a book that determines its success with your preschooler. It is the fact that it is suitable for a child of his age.

(Sometimes this word-for-word memorizing leads un-

PRESCHOOLERS LIKE TO LOOK AT BOOKS

Gesell Institute

wary parents to believe that their boy or girl can read long before this is actually the case. Memorizing is an interesting stage, but it does not constitute true reading.)

But, between four and five, much earlier in some, will come that fascinating time when the child will begin to pick out initial letters or will even ask you, "What does c-a-t spell?" After that, real reading often comes fairly quickly.

Any parent who feels a need to teach any preschooler to read can do her best and most effective work not by prodding a helpless and unready prereader to read. She will make her greatest possible contribution to her child's reading interest and readiness for reading simply by reading aloud.

Reading to a preschooler can be fun for you. For the child, it can provide information, relaxation, fun, familiarity with and interest in books, a time to share with you, and a big first step toward reading himself.

If all this seems too easy a way to foster love of reading and to prepare the child for the time when he, too, will read, this may be a clue to you about much else that works in parenting. Being the successful parent of a preschooler takes much stamina and patience and unselfishness, but it does NOT require vast amounts of equipment, vast expenditures of money (many good books for children now come in paperback and there's always the library!), or vast amounts of technical skill.

We devote a chapter to the importance of reading to your child because it can be so much fun both for you and for him, and also because it is a wonderful way of helping him to appreciate the marvels of everyday life. A rainy day at home, a walk around the neighborhood, the fun of playing with his puppy, seem all the more important, real, and wonderful when he reads about other children who have similar adventures. Your child's here and now will be strengthened and his horizons expanded if you read to him.

Conversely, most children will be better and more enthusiastic readers when the time comes if what they are reading about is at least moderately meaningful to them. One way this can be arranged is if, before they are required to read, they have either had a rather wide experience of living, or *at least* have achieved a good deal of experience vicariously through being read to.

Reading to your child is important because listening to books being read, and eventually looking on as an adult reads to him, constitute the first important steps toward loving books and learning to read to oneself. Though so-called bookless curriculums can be provided for children who find it hard to read, and though many people do live useful and enjoyable lives without doing much reading, customary and conventional success in school, as well as much learning and pleasure in later life, is associated with being an effective and enthusiastic reader.

Just the right book can be so gloriously successful that we shall mention here a handful of those that we and the children we have known have loved the most. For an up-to-date list of favorite books for young children, readers are referred to the revised edition of *Infant and Child in the Culture of Today* (30). However, perhaps your best bet is merely to check with your nearest library or local bookstore. In addition to the perennial old favorites, there is a steady stream of excellent and attractive children's books being made available by all children's book publishers. We suggest that you choose for yourself.

Books for Fun

Fifteen months to two years: At these earliest ages, your best bets are cloth or heavy cardboard books, picturing single familiar objects or domestic animals. Three excellent heavy cardboard books (which can hardly be torn or even bent) are John E. Johnson's *My First Book of Things,* Eloise Wilkins's *Nursery Rhymes,* and Jan Pfloog's *Puppies* (all published by Random House). Or two fine sturdy cloth books are J. P. Miller's *The Cow Says Moo* and Richard Scarry's *Huckle's Book* (Random House). Or try Dorothy Kunhardt's *Pat the Bunny* (Simon & Schuster).

Two years old: There is nothing the typical two-year-old loves more than his new shoes. Thus any book that includes or features *shoes* is bound to be a success. *My Slippers Are Red* by Charlotte Steiner (Knopf) has the added charm of talking about a lot of lovely colors: "My slippers are red, your slippers are blue. We know all the colors. How about you?" Pictures are big and bright; text is short and to the point.

A book that has nicely stood the test of time and that still comes up as a two-year-old's favorite is Margaret Wise Brown's *Goodnight Moon* (Harper & Row). It features the simple, clear illustrations and short one-line-to-a-page text so favored by the very young. It is not only a fun book to read and listen to, but it has helped many a reluctant preschooler to release his tired mother and move on into sleep. Its repetitious theme is soothing: "Good night bears, good night chairs, good night kittens, good night mittens. Good night clocks and good night socks. Good night little house and good night mouse. Good night moon."

Most any 2-year-old will enjoy a wonderful new set of books by Dick Bruna: *The Apple, The Fish, The Little Bird* (Methuen). Or try Rosemary Wells's set which includes *Max's First Word, Max's Toy, Max's New Suit* (Dial).

Two to three years: The important thing about *The Important Book* by Margaret Wise Brown (Harper & Row) is that it tells—and eventually will help your child tell you —what the important thing about a daisy is (it's white), about rain (it's wet), about grass (it's green, it grows, and it smells sweet), and about all sorts of other things in his immediate small world. This is a wonderfully interesting, friendly, informative teaching book. It is safe to say that a book like this, shared between you and your pre-schooler, will do as much, if not more, for his intellectual functioning than all the self-conscious teach-your-pre-schooler books you could possibly buy.

For the two-and-a-half- to three-and-a-half-year-old who just *loves* to hear about when he was a baby and couldn't talk or walk or do all the other wonderful things that he *can* do now, we recommend *Look at Me Now*, one of the new Golden Book series written in co-operation with the Menninger Foundation. Reading this book to-gether can lead you and your child to other fascinating memories of the past and to a proper appreciation of the present, when he *can* do so many things that were impos-sible before.

Three to five years: If, much of the time, your particular preschoolers fight with each other, but if you like to re-member those marvelous occasions when they did get along nicely, you will enjoy Charlotte Zolotow's lovely *Do You Know What I'll Do?* (Harper & Row). This is the enchanting story of a little girl who tells her baby brother about all the nice things she plans to do for him.

"Do you know what I'll do at the seashore? I'll buy a shell to hold the sound of the sea. Do you know what I'll do at the movie? I'll remember the song and sing it to you. Do you know what I'll do when I wake up? I'll remember my dreams and tell them to you. And do you know what I'll do when I grow up and am married? I'll bring you my baby to hug. Like this."

Four years: One of the best and most successful books ever written for the foolish, fun-loving four-year-old is Ruth Krauss's *I Want to Paint My Bathroom Blue* (Harper & Row). This little boy's bathroom is going to be blue, and he tells readers, "I'll make a big white door with a little pink doorknob, and a song about the doorknob goes a doorknob a doorknob a dear little doorknob, a dearknob a dearknob a door little dearknob." If your four-year-old doesn't like this book, we'll eat it.

Four-year-olds love poetry, too. Try yours with Ruth Krauss's *Somebody Else's Nut Tree* (Harper & Row). A little girl finds a nut tree and goes up close and climbs it, and then she sees it is somebody else's nut tree. Other poems are equally nonsensical and amusing.

Or, you can't go wrong with Stoo Hempel's *The Silly Book* (Harper & Row), since silly is the word for the four-year-old.

Four to five year olds: Excellent books for boys and girls of these ages are far too many to list. A few of our own favorites are Robert Benton's *Don't Ever Wish for a Seven Foot Bear* (Knopf), Roger Duvoisin's *Our Veronica Goes to Petunia Farm* (Knopf), Wanda Gag's *Millions of Cats* (Coward McCann), Edith Kessler's *Do Baby Bears Sit on Chairs?* (Doubleday), Shel Silverstein's *The Giving Tree* (Harper & Row).

Books to Help with Feelings

As the world becomes, some feel, increasingly complex and difficult, our means of coping with our difficulties fortunately increase. One of the areas in which we have made rapid advancement is in the area of mental health. To begin with, we now know more about human behavior than ever before. Also, psychological and psychiatric information, advice, and help is available to a much greater extent than formerly. Though much maladjustment and personal unhappiness does still exist, people in general are much freer and much more willing than they used to be to discuss their problems and their feelings. Understanding difficulties often leads to their solution.

Books for preschoolers may seem strange places to look for solutions of personal problems—yet, if you are a preschooler, why not?

Just within the past few years there has been published a substantial number of attractive and interesting books —to be read to the preschooler—about things that might bother him.

Our concern for children is definitely expanding. Consider the matter of thumb sucking. Not too long ago it was generally assumed that children should not suck their thumbs, and that if they did, their parents should try to stop them. So the question parents used to ask was, "How can I stop my child from sucking his thumb?"

Some years later, people asked a different question: "Should I *try* to stop my child from sucking his thumb?"

And now today we have gone a step further. Many now ask themselves, "How does my child feel about his thumb sucking? How can I help him to feel more relaxed about it?"

If thumb sucking is a tensional outlet, as many believe it to be, if the child not only sucks his thumb but *worries* about his sucking, his anxiety, obviously, will make him even more tense. To relieve this anxiety in a preschooler, Kathryn Ernest has written the highly sympathetic story *Danny and His Thumb* (Prentice-Hall).

Danny of this story sucks his thumb much of the time. He likes the way it tastes. He sucks when at the movies, when he goes for a ride, when he has his hair cut. And especially he sucks at night after he has gone to bed. But then, one September day, without anybody doing much about it, after Danny starts school he decides that he doesn't like sucking his thumb as much as he used to.

He doesn't like the hard bump on his thumb. He doesn't like hearing his mother say, "You really shouldn't suck your thumb—it will make your teeth stick out." He notices that his friends don't suck *their* thumbs. And he doesn't have as much TIME to suck as he used to, he is so busy. And he is using his thumb for other important things. So, after a while, he just never thinks about it any more.

Parents have indeed come a long, long way in the last forty years or so as far as attitudes toward thumb sucking. A recent TV moderator asked three sets of parents the following question: "Should your two-year-old be permitted to suck his thumb (1) any time he wants to; (2) only at bedtime; (3) never?" The two younger pairs of parents agreed that a two-year-old should be allowed to suck whenever he wants to. The older pair were firm in their belief that a two-year-old should *never* be allowed to suck.

Two Golden Books, written in co-operation with the Menninger Foundation, give help for other problems that bother many preschoolers. *Sometimes I'm Afraid* by Jane Werner Watson, Robert E. Switzer, M.D., and J. Cotter Hirschberg, M.D., talks about a young child's fears. A three- or four-year-old can be afraid of many things— strangers, or new places, loud noises, the dark, his parents' absence.

But when he gets to know people and places, they are not nearly as scary. Mom and Dad can turn on a light and show him that there's nothing dangerous hiding in the dark. Talking about bad dreams makes them much less frightening. All these scary things are much less threatening when a child can talk them over with his parents. And reading about them together in a friendly book can be just as good as talking.

Sometimes I'm Angry, a companion book, talks about and helps a child to face his angry feelings in an equally sympathetic way. And for all sorts of worries and anxieties, try the comfort of Joan Fassler's *Don't Worry, Dear* (Behavioral Publications), a book dedicated to "every child who ever sucked his thumb, or wet his bed, or stuttered on his words." Its hero, Jerry, is very small and has a lot of problems, but his sympathetic mother assures him: "Don't worry, dear. When you grow bigger you will stay dry all the time. . . . your words will come out better . . . and you won't feel like sucking your thumb any more."

The arrival home of that new baby tends often to be a somewhat traumatic occasion. It may help in your preschooler's adjustment to read with him *The Baby House* by Norma Simon (Lippincott). It tells the story of three mothers—Louise, Lassie, and Mother—and of three fathers, Fuzzy, Lance, and Daddy. And a little girl. All the mothers wanted babies, all the fathers wanted babies, and the little girl wanted all the babies.

The cat mother grew rounder, the dog mother grew rounder, and the little girl's mother grew rounder. Until —all the mothers had their babies, all the fathers had their babies, and the little girl had all the babies. "We loved them, we kissed them, we fed them. We lived in a baby house."

To help the adopted boy or girl understand, and accept, the story of his adoption, you may like an old favorite, revised: *The Chosen Baby*, by Valentina Wasson (Lippincott). Or you may prefer another old favorite, *The Family that Grew*, by Rondell and Michaels (Crown), an attractive pair of books, one for the parents and one for the child.

Or, perhaps best of all, the red, white, and blue *Now We Are a Family* by Judith C. Meredith (Beacon Press). It tells how families come about—some people grow their own babies; some adopt them. It explains that "adopting means doing the mothering and fathering for a baby who was born to someone else."

This very attractive, very helpful book talks about something that earlier books omitted—some of the reasons why a mother and father may not have been able to keep the baby that was born to them. It talks to the child about his natural parents in a sympathetic and frank way, and ends on the positive and supportive note—"We are a family."

And speaking of where babies do come from—young children ask but we suspect that most are not greatly concerned. In this instance it is probably the mother more than the child who needs help. Any well-stocked bookstore or good public library will have many books that discuss the basic facts of sex. The important thing is to find one that *you* like and are comfortable with. If it satisfies you, it is likely to satisfy your boy or girl.

Among good, reliable books giving the basic information necessary for three- to six-year-olds are the following:

How Babies Are Made, by Andrew C. Andry and Steven Schepp (Time-Life); *The Beginning of Life: How Babies Are Born* by Eva Knox Evans (Crowell-Collier); and *The Magic of Life* by Marilyn Schima and Polly Bolian (Prentice-Hall).

Or, if you are especially frank and relaxed about sex yourself, you might like to try *Where Did I Come From?* by Peter Mayle (Lyle Stuart). Better read it first, to be sure you are up to it, before you try it on your child.

One final topic that often arouses much anxiety and that may come into the life of even a preschooler is the topic of death. *Talking about Death,* by Rabbi Earl A. Grollman and illustrated by Gisela Héan (Beacon), is a book so beautiful that the sadness of the subject matter is almost obscured. This is a book that frankly tells the young listener, "When you die, you're dead. Try saying that word, DEAD. It is a hard word to say, isn't it? . . . Dead is dead. It is not a game. It's very real. . . . Grandfather is dead. He will not come back. . . . We cannot see him or talk to him. But we can talk about him and remember him. . . . We can never forget that he died, but we will always remember that he lived."

These are but a few of the best of this rather new kind of book now available that helps with problems for very little boys and girls. We think that such books will prove marvelously useful to many a preschooler over the years.

And when your preschooler grows a little older, you will find other books that can talk to him, helpfully, about things that may be bothering him. Three that we like best are written by psychiatrist Richard A. Gardner. They are: *The Boys and Girls Book about Divorce; Dr. Gardner's Stories about the Real World;* and *The Family Book About Minimal Brain Dysfunction.*

Books to Teach

And finally, lest any reader mistakenly construe our suggestion of "Don't push" as meaning "Don't teach," we should point out that there are now available many splendid books which pleasantly and painlessly will teach the young about almost any subject on earth.

Thus preschoolers can learn about the shapes of things from such attractive books as John Trotter's *Hello! This Is My Shape Book* (Random House), Eric Carle's *My Very First Book of Shapes* (Crowell), or Dr. Seuss's *The Shape of Me and Other Stuff* (Random House).

Colors are even more fun. Try Leo Lionni's *Little Blue and Little Yellow* (Astor Honor) or Eric Carle's *My Very Best Book of Colors* (Crowell) or Richard Hafter's *Colors* (Larousse & Co.)

Sounds tell their own story in Margaret Wise Brown's wonderful series which includes *The Noisy Book, The Indoor Noisy Book, The Seashore Noisy Book* (Harper & Row).

More academic but no less pleasing are the many good books which will teach the eager preschooler how to count, among them Dick Bruna's *I Can Count* (Methuen), Brian Wildsmith's *One, Two, Three* (Watts), Richard Scary's *Best Counting Book Ever* (Random House).

And then of course there are the many ABC books like

Brian Wildsmith's *ABC* (Watts), Roy McKie's *The Alphabet Block Book* (Random House), or Richard Scarry's *ABC Word Book* (Random House).

Good books of nursery rhymes are too many to list, but probably the most fascinating of all is Fitzhugh Dodson's *I Wish I Had A Computer that Makes Waffles* (Oak Tree), which teaches while it entertains. Modern, lively, sometimes ridiculous, it introduces boy or girl to concepts of counting, space, parts of body, times of year and much, much else.

As your child moves on from letters to words, he or she will enjoy such books as *Early Words* or *My First Picture Dictionary* by Richard Scarry (Random House), or *My Very First Words* by Eric Carle (Crowell).

Quite a bit further along the road to reading, good—first to be read to the child and a little later for him to read to himself—is Harper & Row's *I Can Read* series. We especially like *No Fighting, No Biting* by Else Minarik, *Danny and the Dinosaur* by Syd Hoff, and *Last One Home Is a Green Pig* by Edith Hurd.

Truly there are books for every preschooler, no matter what his level or area of interest. And if you start very early to read *to* your child, sooner than you may expect, he or she will be sounding out the words and reading by himself, without any pushing from anybody.

Television

And now we'd like to say a good word for television. When television was new, many parents feared that if their child watched TV it would make him lose interest in reading. This fear was not borne out.

Certainly there are many programs that most parents would not wish their preschoolers to see. Fortunately the young child seems to have better judgment than he is sometimes credited with. If a program is over a child's head, or too violent or exciting, or just not suited to the interests of one his age, his attention span tends to be extremely short.

There are numerous children's programs which even if not superb are at least adequate, harmless, and certainly very much enjoyed. Your child will enjoy them even more if you share some of them with him, laugh together, talk them over. Many preschoolers ask their mothers to watch their favorite programs with them. Why not take the time to do so? Don't try to make every viewing a learning experience. But it will do no harm to teach a lesson now and then. Even a 4- or 5-year-old can respond quite intelligently if you inquire, "Was that a good thing the little boy did?", "What could the Mother have done that would have been nicer?" Both positive and negative happenings on the screen tell their lesson if you take the time to criticize or praise.

And if by chance your preschooler does seem fascinated with some program you consider totally unsuitable— hopefully you have the upper hand. You can forbid the program. Or you can plan his day so that he is not sitting in front of the television set when the program is aired.

It isn't necessary for children to be usefully occupied through all hours of the day. Though many speak scathingly of the idea of using television as a baby-sitter, there are many tired mothers who are delighted to be able to call on it to fill just that role.

Our feeling has always been that if you don't want your young child to watch some of the things on the air, just arrange that he doesn't watch them. And for those parents who complain that they cannot control their youngster's television watching—we would say that the problem is more one of discipline than of TV.

A particular use of television we question is one that is commonly much lauded—its use to *teach* the young child his letters and numbers, to teach him how to match shapes, to speed up his so-called cognitive development.

It does no harm for a preschooler to learn his letters or numbers or shapes and sounds if he so wishes and if it is his own spontaneous idea. Certainly it pleases those around him and does give him the idea that learning can be fun. It is merely important for parents not to confuse facile rote performance with readiness for formal schooling at an age below that which law and custom usually allow.

Talking with Your Child

Reading to children is fun and it is important. But even before the time you will read to him, and during that time and after that time, a more important activity than reading is talking with your child.

Those who advise parents about their teenagers emphasize that the most important thing you can do in helping a teenager stay on the right track is to communicate with him.

Communication should not wait to start until your child has something fascinating to say. It should start even before his first syllables. Talk to your *baby* about all sorts of interesting things. This may sound foolish to outsiders, but it won't sound foolish to your baby.

When he starts to "da-da," repeat what he says and encourage him to say more. When he gets to the jargon and short-sentence stage, be interested, be responsive. And all through the preschool years, when you're often tired and your offspring's every utterance has lost its total charm, keep right on talking, and encourage him to talk.

Conversing with your boy or girl at any age can be one of your best techniques, not only for encouraging the relationship between you, but also—if you are concerned about his thinking and his mind—one of the best ways to encourage him to think and to react in a vivid way to the world around him.

Talking requires no purchased equipment, no special time or place. It is always available and one of your best bets in raising a happy, confident, intelligent, self-expressive child. If YOU find what he says interesting, it will help him to think of himself as an interesting person who has something worthwhile to say.

9 / Mind Does Matter

Books that tell young parents how to make their children smart abound, and new ones are constantly being published. Among those which promise the most, in case you wish to and think you can make your boy or girl brighter than Nature originally intended, are: *How to Raise Your Child's I.Q.* by David Engler (Criterion Press), *How to Teach Your Baby to Read* by Glenn Doman (Random House)—or even more unusual, *Teach Your Baby Math* also by Glenn Doman (Simon & Schuster)—and *Teach Your Baby* by Genevieve Painter (Simon & Schuster).

Of these books, and others like them, psychiatrist Jerome Fass has commented that all they do is:

Make the writers richer.
Make you poorer.
Make you a boastful bore at social gatherings.
Give your child something to forget.
Give your child the beginning of an emotional block toward learning.

And the *Saturday Review* once remarked succinctly that "Joan Beck's *How to Raise a Brighter Child* reminds us of How to Raise a Bigger Begonia."

One further title has been added to the already too-long list. Sparkman and Carmichael have come out with a

Blueprint for a Brighter Child (69). Actually, this book includes some helpful suggestions about good things you can do with your preschooler to help you enjoy him and help him enjoy life and get the most out of daily living. It does *not* provide a blueprint for a brighter child.

When intelligence tests are given to Head Start and other presumably culturally deprived children, before such children have had any appreciable experience with pencil and paper and/or a school environment, and then repeated after an interval during which the children did have some academic or culturally enriching opportunity, a second I.Q. score has often been found to be higher than the first.

This was of course encouraging, especially to researchers. It did not necessarily mean that the so-called intervention (the teaching or training given the child) made him brighter than he was to start with. It meant simply, in our opinion, that he did better in the testing situation. And in many instances children were not able to continue rating at the higher level; scores all too often reverted to or toward their original level.

A child's inherited intellectual level is probably a range rather than a specific point. What happens to him in life largely determines whether he will function at or near his top potential or at or near his lowest potential. This potential range is probably as much as ten or fifteen I.Q. points.

Certainly it is important for all of us, in both the school and home, to give every child the best and richest and most stimulating atmosphere and environment possible. We do this with the hope of permitting him to function at his fullest. We should not do it with the expectation of making him more intelligent than he was born to be.

In a clinical practice, as well as in research, we have found intelligence scores to be, in general, remarkably stable. In one research study of our own, thirty-three children were examined in infancy on Gesell Infant Behavior tests, and forty-four more children were examined in the preschool years on the Gesell preschool scale. All subjects were checked at ten years of age with the WISC full scale examination.*

Early examination results were found to be highly predictive of the ten-year-old response. Twenty-one of the thirty-three infants, or 63.6 per cent, had scores in infancy that fell within ten points of the ten-year I.Q. score. Sixteen (48.5 per cent) fell within five points. The average age for the first examination was thirty-three weeks.

In forty of forty-four preschoolers (91 per cent) preschool and ten-year scores fell within ten points of each other; in twenty-one (48 per cent) within five points. The average age of the first preschool examination for this group was 25.5 months.

These findings clearly indicate a rather great consistency of expressed intelligence level over eight- to ten-year periods. However, obviously such scores remain most stable when a child remains in a fairly stable environment and when, hopefully, things go reasonably well for him right along. A poor environment, illness, terribly upset living conditions, can and often do depress any child's level of functioning.

Thus it is not too unusual for us to examine a child who *looks* to us potentially quite normal who nevertheless rates below normal on an intelligence test. If our own judgment of a child's potential differs markedly from the way he measures (that is, if he looks normal or bright but tests in the dull normal or retarded range) we label him as "unclassified" or as having a "depressed I.Q." This merely means that in our expectation, when things in his living straighten out—when (if he has no family of his

*Louise B. Ames, "Predictive Value of Infant Behavior Examinations," in *Exceptional Infant: The Normal Infant,* vol. 1 (Seattle: Special Child Publications, 1967).

own) he can be put into a better home, or his own home conditions improve, or when his health or visual functioning are improved—then he will on a subsequent examination score much higher than he did on the first.

If and when this happens, and it often does happen, we do not consider that we or his parents or his school have "increased his intelligence" or "made him brighter." We figure merely that what we have done is to see that the conditions in his living are such that he can express himself at his best.

However, this does not mean from a practical view that a child necessarily needs to change his environment to improve his intellectual functioning. You as a parent can, right in your own home and without doing anything specially "intellectual" do your best to see that your boy or girl is comfortable and happy and provided with a normally rich, full, and stable environment. When you do this, his or her functioning in all areas, including the intellectual, will usually be at its best.

It is important to remember that children grew up bright, happy, capable, and effective, successful in school and later on in adult life long before anybody had ever talked about *cognitive development.* Your parents and ours, quite naturally and unself-consciously did things that undoubtedly stimulated intellectual functioning. People then did them for the fun of it, not because they were concerned with cognitive development.

Most parents, naturally and for their own interest and pleasure, answer their young children's many questions, talk to them, read to them, play with them, take them for walks and trips, tell them stories, explain things to them, because they enjoy doing these things as a normal part of living.

Many parents, also, take great pleasure in teaching their children to build with blocks, to manipulate jigsaw puzzles, to count, to name their colors, or identify the letters on their alphabet blocks, to say little rhymes or to sing little songs. Most of us feel pride and pleasure when our youngster can first count or recite the alphabet.

It is a customary and natural part of parenthood to enjoy teaching the young. But teaching is not pushing. Enjoying and encouraging your child's normal intellectual or academic endeavours is a normal part of being a parent.

You don't have to worry whether or not you are doing it all "right." And you don't do these things in an effort to increase your child's intelligence. A young father recently admitted, "Our daughter doesn't pay a lot of attention to all these 'learning materials' we bought her. She just likes to play with her toys."

The fact that we don't worry about your child's mind by no means implies that we are not interested in it. And obviously *you* are going to be. Fortunately it does not require a specialist or any special techniques to keep you informed about how things are going with your child's thinking.

Your best ways to keep abreast of what is going on are to talk with your child, listen to him, notice how he reacts. One extremely pleasurable way of sharing in your child's intellectual development is to take part in his or her imaginative play.

Parents are often amazed at the tremendous amount of imagination which goes into most any preschooler's play. Blocks become people or animals or teacups; dolls "talk" and go through the child's own daily routines; totally invisible companions appear and play unique games with your child.

Or the child himself or herself takes the part of other people. One little four-year-old girl we knew pretended she was two of her nursery school teachers playing school, only one of them didn't want to play.

Some of this imaginative play is rather private and special to the child and his contemporaries. But most are delighted if a grown-up will take part. Imaginative play with your child can be one of your best ways of encouraging his own imagination, and for the most part requires almost no equipment or expense.

Another good way of finding out what is going on in the young child's mind is to ask him or her to tell you a story. You may be surprised to discover what good stories your youngster can tell. Even a two-year-old if mature for his age and fairly verbal can tell you a short story, such as:

Baby. She cries. She crawls. She cries some more. She has some breakfast. No toast. Her Mummy puts her to bed.

By four years of age a typical story will be more elaborate and will involve more action and probably more violence.*

Don't grab anything from toys when children have them. Balloons you blow up and sometimes they break. If the ants eat your house and break the stones and make holes in the stairs 'cause they want to live there, you can't get into the house. If you eat food and throw the dishes, they break and you get spanked. You throw them and cut yourself and your arm and then you bleed. If you throw books, you get spanked by somebody you don't know.

There are many other simple, everyday ways in which you can, if you wish, check on how your child's mind is developing. You can observe how far he seems to have come in relation to the ordinary ideas about time, space, size, shape, and number—all the concepts that combine to allow a child to understand the world around him.

As you watch your child develop through the various stages outlined here, you will realize that you do provide

*In stories collected by us (Louise B. Ames, "Children's Stories," *Genetic Psychology Monographs*, 73, 1966, pp. 337–396) the outstanding theme at all ages, but increasing with age, was violence.

many of the basic ideas; you do give reasonable help and assistance. But you will also appreciate that the child learns about these things and understands them *in his own time,* when he is ready, and not at the time *you* decide. You can teach or push all you want to, but the usual two- or even three-year-old tends to have a rather limited notion of any of these basic concepts.

We give below the times at which one may expect, on the average, that concepts of time, space, size, shape, and number develop.

Sense of Time

The development of a sense of time proceeds as follows from eighteen months to five years.

Eighteen Months: The child lives in the present and has little if any sense of past or future. He cannot wait. No time words are used by him, but he responds to the word "now." He has some slight sense of timing—he may roll a ball and wait for it to stop before pursuing it. The sight of food may bring him to the table.

Twenty-one Months: The child still lives chiefly in the present. His chief time word is still "now." Projection into the future begins to come in, in that he may wait in response to "in a minute." There is an improved sense of timing. Two children may rock in rhythm.

Two Years: An important advance takes place at this age. Though the child still lives very much in the present, several words that denote future time come in: "gonna," "in a minute." He will wait in response to such words as "wait," and "soon."

Two-and-a-Half Years: The child now freely uses words implying past, present, and future time. For the present, he may say "day," "morning," "afternoon." For the future, "some day," "one day," "tomorrow," "pretty soon."

Past time is usually designated by "last night." He may freely use names of the days of the week, although inaccurately.

Three Years: More new time words come in during the six months from two-and-a-half to three years than in any other similar time interval. Past, present, and future are referred to, and he now knows "yesterday." There are still more words for expressing the future than the past, but the child may talk nearly as much about past and future as about present.

He knows expressions of duration: "all the time," "all day," and "for two weeks." There is a pretense of telling time, usually inaccurate. But the word "time" is often used: "What time?" "It's time," "lunchtime."

The child of three can tell how old he is, when he goes to bed (in terms of some other activity), and what he will do tomorrow. However, he may answer all questions about time with some one inappropriate clock time or with some number such as "fifty-nine."

Three-and-a-Half Years: Great variety of expressions indicating past, present, and future now are used spontaneously and mostly accurately. Child uses many complicated expressions of duration: "for a long time," "for years," and "for a whole week." Or he uses such phrases as "two things at once." There is not so much an increase in number of time words as in refinement of use: "It's almost time," and "a nice long time." The child expresses habitual action, as "on Fridays," and may refer to future happenings as in the past: "I'm going to take a nap yesterday."

Four Years: Past, present, and future words continue to be used freely and about equally. Many new time words are added here. The word "month" comes in; also such broad concepts as "next summer" and "last summer." The child seems to have a reasonably clear understanding of when events of the day take place in relation to each other. He is spontaneously speedy but slows down if pushed.

Five Years: Most of the time words commonly used by adults are now in the child's vocabulary. The child can tell what day it is, can name the days of the week in correct order, and can tell (for example) what day follows Sunday. He knows his age and can project forward to tell how old he will be at his next birthday.

He is interested in clocks though most five-year-olds still cannot tell time. He is also interested in calendars and likes to find birthday and holiday dates.

Sense of Space

The growing child's sense of space develops from one year to six years as follows.

One Year: The child gestures for "up," wriggles for "down," but does not have the words.

Fifteen Months: The child can say "up" and mean it.

Eighteen Months: Such space words as "down," "off," "bye-bye," and "all gone" are now part of the child's vocabulary. Out for a walk, he runs ahead of the adult and explores byways. In a test situation he can obey two directions with a ball; that is, can put it on a chair and can give it to his mother when so directed. But no space words are used yet in answering questions.

Twenty-one Months: Space words used now include "up," "down," "on," "off." Also he uses effectively the words "all gone" and "here." The space he lives in, as at eighteen months, is definitely here and now. The child wants what he wants when he wants it.

Two Years: Although two is not a particularly expansive age, an enlarging concept of space is indicated by the use of such words as "there," "where," "other side," "outdoors," "upstairs," and "up high." The more complex notion of container and contained comes in with the words "in" and "out." "In" is the most-used space word; "all gone" is also prominent. The child can also ask space questions: "Where is Mummy?"

He can obey four directions with a ball in a test situation: can put it on a chair, on a table, give it to Mother, and give it to the examiner. Out for a walk, he likes to walk on curbs and walls.

Two-and-a-Half Years: At this age there is a very strong sense of space. The child likes to have things in their exact places and does not like change. Many of his space words reflect this rigidity. He says "right," "right here," "right up there," "right home," "right down." Also he now combines two space words to give more exactness to location: "way up," "in here," "under the table." A wider space than earlier is covered by the words "near" and "far" or "far away."

More new space words are added between two and two-and-a-half years than in any other six-month age period. (Most of the new time words come in between two-and-a-half and three years.)

There is a great interest in having things in their proper places, and he may help put things away. Out for a walk, he begins to think of destination.

Three Years: New space words used here suggest a refined notion of space: "back," "corner," "over," "from," "by," "up on top." There is more interest in detail and direction. A superior child may explain that you "turn right." Asked where he sleeps, the three-year-old no longer says merely, "In my crib," but may tell about his bedroom as well.

Three can tell what street he lives on but not the number. He can put a ball under or on a chair. He can also carry out commands that involve understanding such words as "over," "crooked," "big," "high," "long," and "tall."

Out for a walk, he definitely has a destination in mind and may like always to follow the same route. However, he may still not be good at judging distance and may bump into things.

Three-and-a-Half Years: "Next to" and "between" mark increased interest in new dimensions of space. The child uses "go" (meaning belong) and "find," to express interest in appropriate places for objects. "Way down," "way off," "way far" express expanding and also exact interest in location.

If asked how he gets to a certain place, he will answer "on the bus" or "in the car." He cannot tell by what route.

Four Years: Not too many new space words, but much use of expansive words as: "far away," "way up there," and "way off." A new dimension is suggested in use of "behind."

The child can now tell his street and city. He can, on command, put a ball on, under, in front of, and in back of a chair. He enjoys playing hide-and-seek; can go on errands outside the house if no street crossing is required, and likes to visit neighbors. Out for a walk, he runs ahead of the adult and can wait at a crossing. If asked how to get to a certain place, he may try to describe the route, though he is more likely to say "the goat way" or "by the ball place."

Five Years: The child of five is here and now, very literal and factual, very focal. He likes to remain close to home base, close to Mother. Also he likes to have things placed neatly and close beside each other. He is primarily interested in his home and immediate neighborhood, not in faraway things.

He likes to run errands around the house. Most five-year-olds can cross streets that have traffic lights, and go to kindergarten alone. The child can now carry out commands in regard to "few," "forward," "backward," "tiny," "smooth," and "high." He may enjoy tracing simple journeys on maps and may indicate specific landmarks. He is interested in the space that is here but not much interested in spatial relations.

The child is interested in distant cities and states if he knows someone there. He likes to go on excursions with his mother.

Six Years: The child's environment is expanding and now includes relationships between home, neighborhood, school, and expanding community. The child himself is the center of his own universe, but he shows much interest in the sun, moon, and planets.

He is less focal than at five and is now interested, for example, in the whole schoolroom. Most six-year-olds can distinguish left and right on their own body but not on the bodies of others. Some can tell points of compass from a familiar starting point or can name streets near home.

Sense of Size and Shape

Now let us look at the development of the sense of size and shape from twenty-one months to six years of age.

Twenty-one Months: When presented with a form-board with round, square, and triangular holes and forms to fit these holes, the child can successfully fit two of the forms into the correct holes. He spontaneously uses the word "big."

Two-and-a-Half Years: He can place all three blocks in formboard holes correctly and can, with only initial error, put them in correctly after the board has been rotated. He can also match one of five color forms correctly.

Three Years: Can identify by pointing four out of ten of the usual geometric forms (square, circle, oval, etc.). (The child is asked to point to one on a card, like the sample given him.) The three-year-old matches three of five color forms correctly. He has made great progress in perception of form in everyday things.

He can ride a tricycle through a small door without bumping.

Three-and-a-Half Years: The child can match all of five color forms, can now point correctly to six of the usual ten geometric forms, and his interest in comparative size is expressed by such words as "littlest" and "bigger."

Four Years: Now the child can point correctly to eight of ten geometric forms. But he still, in everyday life, confuses relation of sizes of things, as button and buttonhole. Also he still misjudges his own size in relation to an object.

Five Years: Now he can point correctly to all ten of the ten usual geometric forms. The five-year-old is learning the meaning of "big," "bigger," and "biggest."

Sense of Number and Arithmetic

From one year to six years the child's sense of number and arithmetic develops as follows:

One Year: The characteristic infant behavior of handling one object after another, as one block after another, is the groundwork for later counting.

Eighteen Months: Such words as "more car," or "more cooky" suggest some notion of plurality.

Two Years: The child uses plurals to designate more than one, or he may say "two balls" or "anudder."

Two-and-a-Half Years: He may want "one for each hand," or he can give "just one" of something on request.

Three Years: The child can give "just one" or "just two." He can count two objects and he may be reported by his mother to be able to count to five.

Four Years: The four-year-old child can count three objects, pointing correctly to each as he counts. He understands "bigger." But note that even though he can count three, or even four objects, it will usually be at least six months more before he can answer the question, "How many?"

Four-and-a-Half Years: The child can correctly give "just one," "just two" or "just three." He can count, with correct pointing, four objects and can then answer the question "How many?" He may be reported by his mother to count to ten. He understands such terms as "most" and "both" but not the terms "same" and "equal."

Five Years: The five-year-old can count thirteen objects with correct pointing. He can count by ones, usually stopping at nineteen or twenty-nine. He can write a few numbers but may not be able to identify what he has written. And he can tell correctly how many fingers he has on one hand.

Five-and-a-Half Years: The child now counts twenty-one objects with correct pointing and can give correct total when asked "How many?" He may be able to write numbers one to ten, but there are many reversals. He can add correctly within five but may need to use his fingers.

Six Years: The child counts by ones to thirty or more and may count by tens to one hundred and by fives to about fifty. He may be able to write numbers up to twenty but still with some reversals. He can add within ten and subtract within five. He is interested in balanced numbers as two and two, three and three.

Though Harvard psychologist Jerome Bruner has stated, and apparently still maintains, that any child can be taught almost any subject in some appropriate way at any time, this statement seems to many of us far-fetched.

The story goes that when the famed Swiss psychologist Jean Piaget was asked by an American reporter if he agreed with Professor Bruner's statement, he replied, "Only an American would ask." Whether this story is true or not, it is true that the question "Can you teach any child almost anything at any time?" is called in Europe "the American question."

Piaget has, through the years, in both Europe and

America, achieved great popularity and respect because of his writings about the development of the child's mind, or his so-called cognitive development. He has pointed out, correctly, that the child's thinking grows and develops in a patterned, predictable way, just as do his other behaviors.

Piaget's basic philosophy is very similar to our own, as first proposed by Dr. Arnold Gesell. He stresses that behavior is based primarily on physical structure and develops in a patterned way, influenced but not determined by environmental factors.

Where Piaget and Gesell differ is that Piaget gives great emphasis to the mind and thinking as such. Gesell, on the other hand, used to insist that "mind manifests itself" in almost *any* behavior. He felt that even in earliest infancy, even simple actions, such as looking at an object, or reaching for an object, or smiling at Mother or Father, were examples of the mind in action. A child does not have to talk or write to tell us that he is thinking.

This is important for parents of young children to know. You need not feel that you are neglecting your preschooler's mind or his intellectual development if you are not teaching him to recognize letters and numbers or to read and write. You are teaching him all through the day, by almost everything you do. There is much to be learned in life besides formal school subjects.

However, not all minds are alike and not all thinking is alike. Not only are some individuals potentially much more intelligent than others, but some individuals are better able to think abstractly than are others.

It is generally recognized that there is a big difference between so-called concrete thinking (thinking about objects and things) and abstract thinking (thinking about ideas and relationships). Piaget puts the ability to think abstractly as beginning around seven years of age. That is, even potentially abstract thinkers do not start out thinking abstractly—they have to arrive at that ability.

The point is that some individuals never arrive at the place where they are doing any very substantial amount of abstract thinking. (You, yourselves, undoubtedly know some people who talk about nothing but people and things, activities and events; others who, more abstractly, like to discuss the meaning of things or the ideas behind certain actions.)

The most customary terms for these two kinds of thinking are concrete and abstract. The California psychologist Arthur Jensen describes them as Level I and Level II thinking. Jensen suggests, correctly, that most necessary school subjects can be taught at a Level I (concrete) level even if a child may not have yet developed, or may never be going to develop, any substantial amount of Level II (abstract) thinking.

Thus he proposes that education should not wait for, or should not depend upon, more complex or abstract thinking. He maintains that every child, regardless of the level or quality of his thinking, deserves the right to an adequate education.

In the preschool years all of this will not yet have become a tremendous problem except that it is important, fairly early, to anticipate and accept the fact that some children, children capable of growing up to be perfectly adequate human beings, are not going to be great thinkers and may never be tremendously successful at the conventional kind of schooling.

Of such children people often say, "He (she) is going to be much better at living than at learning." Low grades in school are not necessarily a signal of ultimate failure in life.

In the past there has been a rather widely accepted notion that boys and men tend to be better at abstract thinking than girls and women. Women's Liberation, of course, staunchly denies this difference. Now that we are more open to the possibility that women may in many respects be "equal" to men, it is going to be interesting to see if reality contradicts the traditional notion.

All of this clearly leads to the fact that you do NOT need to teach your baby to read. You do not even need to teach your preschooler to read. We have emphasized that we are very, very much in favor of your reading *to* your preschooler and of having him listen and enjoy. All in good season will come the time when he will look on as you read, will ask what initial letters stand for, will eventually spell out some series of letters as H O T or S T O P and will ask what they spell.

It is NOT necessary to put up little cards around the house with the letters A, B, C (etc.) or the numbers 1, 2, 3 (etc.) on them. It is not necessary to label the cat C A T, or the dog D O G. Your baby doesn't need to know that C A T is the name of his pet. Even your preschooler doesn't need to know. (Though if you enjoy doing these things and don't expect too much to come of them, probably they don't do any harm.) Along about four or five years of age, chances are your child will be interested in this kind of thing. He won't be any further ahead when this time comes because you have labeled things earlier.

All of this does *not* mean that you should *not* permit even a very young child to read. If your three- or four-year-old happens to be so advanced in the reading department that he or she *wants* to read—of course you should permit it. We have met mothers so convinced that they should not push their preschooler (an attitude which obviously we commend) that they believe they should not even *allow* a preschooler to read!

By no means is that what we recommend. Let your child decide, and if he wants to read, let him!

All we have said does not mean that we do not respect or think highly of intellectual functioning. It is merely that in our opinion your child's thinking, like his walking and talking, will develop all in its own good time. We do not especially separate his thinking from his walking and talking and toilet training, or his getting along, or not getting along, with other children.

Growing up is all of a piece. For practical purposes, or for teaching or research, we often speak separately about the different kinds of behavior. But it is a single, unitary child who is growing up.

If he is well endowed, if you, his parents, take a reasonable interest in him, if you provide him with a normal surrounding in which to grow up, and if you pay as much attention to him as does the ordinary parent, his mind will take care of itself. You do not need to provide special cognitive materials or methods to assure that a normally endowed child will grow up bright, effective, intelligent.

10/
Mind Not All
That Matters

There are many ways of pushing a child, but when people talk about pushing a preschooler, they are generally thinking about his MIND. They are considering whether or not they should teach him to read, whether or not to do something or other that will increase his intelligence.

It is perhaps natural that people should worry about minds and intelligence since, in general, it has been believed (whether correctly or not) that the more intelligent a person is, the better he will do at living.

Yet chances are that the most useful and effective thing a parent can do for a young boy or girl is not to try to increase that child's intelligence, but to recognize and accept it pretty much as it is, and to govern one's expectations accordingly. Evidence is largely lacking of any marked and sustained increases in intelligence brought about by parental or other efforts.

But there is much more to any child's equipment than just his mind, and there are many fields of behavior other than the so-called cognitive in which some parents inadvisedly and ineffectively do push.

Eating behavior: Perhaps nothing in the world has been pushed more vigorously and more fruitlessly than food. Many parents believe that their children need more food, and a wider variety of food, than most children will eat. (On the other hand, sometimes the kinds of food they push most do not make up an ideal diet, as we have emphasized in Chapter 6.)

There is certainly no surer way of producing a feeding problem than pushing food; no better way of encouraging a child to eat and to enjoy his food than saying very little about it.

Fortunately most parents have learned this lesson well. Also, parents today appreciate the fact that some children have large appetites, some small. They have discovered that as a rule a hungry child, unpressed, will eat enough to keep him not only alive but reasonably healthy.

Child specialists and pediatricians hear much less today than formerly about the child who "just won't eat a bite." It used to be the number one problem in many households. No more.

Sleeping: A hungry child, as a rule, will eat. A sleepy child will not always sleep. More than that, some preschoolers seem almost to lack any "reasonable" need for sleep. (One often *hears,* especially from grandmothers, of that satisfactory preschooler who says, "Johnny's sleepy. Johnny wants to go to bed." One less often *sees* this remarkable creature.)

As a rule, it is safe to say that in most households parents do understandably try to push their children into more sleep than those children care about.

Very early in infancy, and with some children right up through three years of age, a daytime nap is accepted quite willingly. After that, there is often less sleepiness and more resistance to the notion of a nap. Fortunately, most (though not all) will accept a play nap in their room if they are not required to sleep or stay in bed. Such a nap brings welcome relief to Mother and gives the child a chance to rest and recuperate from his own activity.

Sleeping at night is the difficult time, and actually it is bedtime and release into sleep rather than the sleep itself that usually causes the trouble. This is one routine where you DO have to push. Most parents of preschoolers want the evenings to themselves, and we assume that young children need a certain amount of sleep.

Getting preschoolers to bed isn't always easy. It may help to know some of the things you'll be up against.

The mother whose infant, or fifteen-to-twenty-four-monther, has gone to bed right along without objection, and has fallen asleep easily and comfortably, is often disconcerted when, around two years of age, bedtime becomes suddenly more difficult. Instead of settling down contentedly into easy sleep, the boy or girl suddenly finds it difficult to let mother go.

Even after she is out of the room, he calls her back with seemingly endless demands for "drink of water," "potty," "kiss." Some of these demands represent real needs—he may actually feel the need to urinate once again or he really may be thirsty.

As likely as not, though, the demands—however they may be expressed—are really for mother's continued presence. And if she gives in, if he finds that his will is stronger than hers, that his need for her continued presence is greater than her need to get away, his demands may continue through the entire evening.

Best if you can combine compassion with firmness, the exact proportions of each depending on your own patience and the strength of your child's demands. A good balance is not easy to achieve, but the time of evening does come when Mother or Father will need to say, "That's all," and mean it.

By two-and-a-half the persistent but random bedtime demands may have solidified into the need for a formal and ever-repeated ritual: bath, teeth brushed, play with Daddy on the rug, two stories—always the same—then a goodnight hug and kiss.

The mother who still has the strength and patience to

give herself fully to this ritual without expressing a natural impulse to cut it short and escape, often finds that she saves time in the long run. It almost seems that the more you give in this situation, the more you get. The final step of your getting away may be made part of the ritual: "And then Jimmy closes his eyes and gives Mummy a big hug, and then Mummy goes out into the living room and Jimmy goes to sleep."

Probably the majority of parents do at least attempt to set up a regular 7 to 8 o'clock bedtime, even for these hard-to-get-to-bed two-and-a-half year olds. A few, realizing that sleep needs vary tremendously from child to child, allow a later-than-average bedtime. This admittedly extends the parents' child-caring day, but does make bedtime when it finally comes a lot easier. A sleepy child obviously is easier to put to bed than one who is wide awake and full of pep.

Around three years of age, many children are better able to release their mother at bedtime, and sleep comes more easily than earlier. Now nighttime problems may come in the middle of the night, when some find it hard to stay asleep and stay in bed till morning. In fact, wakefulness is common, and at this time many begin (if permitted) a rather vigorous night life. Some get out of their crib, go to the bathroom, go downstairs, get some food and "read" a book in the living room. Such a child may be found asleep on the couch in the morning.

Others are content to play or talk to themselves in bed for a while or to get out of bed and play in their room till sleepy. Others may insist on getting into the parents' bed.

Realizing that it is not possible to force a child to stay asleep if he is wakeful, many parents try to arrange it that the child's night waking will not disturb others in the family. A light that the child can reach, simple (quiet) toys and some unmessy food, such as peanuts, carrot sticks, or raisins, serve to keep many contented in their own room.

Tying the door loosely closed so that the child cannot roam around the house and get into trouble may be necessary. Taking the child into your own bed, unless he is one who breaks habits easily and quickly, may lead to many undesirable complications.

Elimination: Nowhere more than in the important area of elimination has the wisdom of the modern parent made itself evident.

Earlier in the century, parent and pediatrician combined, in a climax of environmental thinking, to urge young infants to ever greater achievement in the way of becoming completely toilet trained. Some parents went so far as to claim that their four- or six-month babies were already "trained." Pediatricians and other child specialists applauded.

We now appreciate that it was the parent, not the infant, who was trained. A careful and lucky mother might indeed have managed to combine baby and pot much of the time at the exact moment when the baby was about to void. He was no more trained than that.

Such early "successes," in most instances, gave way to later irregularity. And then the mothers of these seemingly precocious babies started to push. How could an infant who "succeeded" in staying dry and/or clean at thirty weeks, fail at forty?

Happily, the falseness of this entire position—if you started soon enough and pushed hard enough you could outdo all your friends and neighbors and have the earliest-trained baby on the block—soon became apparent.

Relaxed mothers today appreciate that it takes a good number of months, or even years, before the average boy or girl is fully ready to be dry and clean in the daytime, let alone dry at night.

Outmoded pushing has given way to a marvelously relaxed attitude on the part of many young mothers today (if not always on the part of *their* mothers!). Most now appreciate that they will save everybody time and trouble if they delay any vigorous efforts to toilet train until their offspring shows at least some readiness to respond to such efforts.

Many a young mother today will tell you: "I waited till he was almost two. Then I noticed that the time between one wet diaper and the next was getting longer, and he often woke up dry after his nap. So I began to try to 'catch' him, and the first thing you knew, he had practically trained himself."

Most important of all is not to push night dryness. Some children are able to stay dry all night (with, perhaps, the help of a pickup for toileting around ten o'clock or when parents go to bed) at a surprisingly early age. Many others, perfectly normal boys and girls, are not ready to stay dry all night till they are five or six years of age, or even older.

By the time your child is six or seven, if you are, quite naturally, becoming impatient with night wetting, or if it upsets *him,* you will be well justified to check with your doctor to be sure that nothing is physically wrong. And then if it isn't, you may wish to try one of the several excellent and relatively inexpensive so-called conditioning devices now on the market.* These devices consist merely of a special small sheet of material so treated that a battery-operated buzzer rings when the material is dampened. At first, it is the buzzer that wakes the child, but soon he becomes conditioned, so that a full bladder alone is enough to waken him. They can be, and often are, remarkably effective in helping boy or girl take that final step that insures night dryness.

Enuresis (bed-wetting past the usual time of dryness)

*Among the devices that we have found most effective, all around $50, are Dry-O-Matic, which can be ordered from the Dry-O-Matic Company, 10055 Nadine, Huntington Woods, Michigan 48070; Utrol, distributed by J. G. Shuman Associates, Inc., Box 306, Scotch Plains, New Jersey 07076; or, for Canada, Dry Bed Products, P.O. Box 6169, Postal Station G, Vancouver 8, B.C., Canada.

does run in families. Though you will still want to do what you can to help your child stay dry at night, it may help you understand and sympathize with a child's later-than-usual night wetting if you check and find that members of your own or your spouse's family were also late in achieving night dryness.

Tensional outlets: In today's possibly less demanding and certainly more realistic culture, an increasing number of parents, with the blessings of their pediatrician or their child-guidance specialist, are willing for the often tense young person to find expression for that tension without prohibition or punishment.

It was not too long ago that the average parent inquired, "How can I stop my child from sucking his thumb?" "How can I get that old rag of a blanket away from him?" "What shall I do about his bottle? He's two years old and he still wants a bottle at bedtime."

It was then considered a matter of discipline. If your child sucked his thumb, fondled his blanket, clung to his bottle, you considered that he had a "bad habit" and that you must break that habit.

Today most of us, parents and specialists alike, think of all these little things that children do as tensional outlets. We think not of how these behaviors can be stopped or prevented but of why the child feels these tensions and of how we can help him to feel less tense so that he will no longer need these particular outlets and comforts.

We work and feel with the child, not against him. We are his friends and sympathizers, not his enemies and disciplinarians. Most of us no longer push our child out of or away from his needed tensional outlets. We think more in terms of helping him to the place where ritualized outlets for tension will not be needed any more.

Socializing: As we shall emphasize in Chapter 13, we see nursery school as an opportunity for the child to learn about himself and his relationship to others, rather than a place for academic instruction. This attitude holds even more true of the young child at home.

Assuming that you have more than one child in your family, a large part of your time will be employed in helping them get on with each other (12). That is a book in itself. Enough to say here that helping young children to learn to live with, and hopefully to love, each other is quite as important as any attempt to encourage their intellectual growth.

The 4-year-old who said to his little brother, "Please, Bobby dear, let me play with the truck now," had been taught well, by a mother who had suggested to him that asking nicely sometimes brings the best results.

And here as in other areas, you do not get too far by pushing. The ordinary 2½-year-old, for instance, is not yet ready to share or to play cooperatively. Six months of added age may help him more in this direction than any amount of admonition or instruction.

Discipline: Speaking of discipline—don't you need to push here? Certainly most children do not do all the "proper" things that we require of their own accord.

So, don't we have to push? Possibly. But not too tremendously much during the preschool years. Eventually, one hopes, your child will come to the place where he or she hangs up clothes, keeps his or her room clean, tells the truth, *wants* to share family tasks. It will not be during the preschool years. And though your admonition and example may speed these things up slightly, that big push from you must have time on its side to bring about success.

We as parents discipline our children primarily in order that they will one day discipline themselves. But the transfer of responsibility from you to them comes very slowly, often painfully. Hard work and patience on your part, maturity on theirs, are required. No big push from you will do the trick until and unless it is combined with readiness and maturity on the part of your child.

Whether it is a matter of daily routines, of discipline, of manners and morals or of the child's *mind,* most child specialists today have adopted a very strong *Don't Push* approach. They do not push solid foods; they do not push weaning; they do not push walking; they do not push early toilet training; they do not push termination of thumb sucking.

Sometimes it seems that we are slow to learn our lessons about how best to live with and to deal with our children. But, except in the realm of intellectual function, most of us *have* learned that each child has his own timetable and that we do not get far by pushing.

Only the intellectual seems currently a matter of over-concern, and with regard to the intellectual we might paraphrase James Thurber and advise all parents to "let their minds alone."

11 / Common Problems and What to Do About Them

The fact that we sound rather relaxed on the subject of bringing up preschoolers, and reasonably confident that your own will survive and turn out favorably, does not mean that there is never anything for parents to be concerned about.

Most parents do worry, quite a good deal, as they raise their children. Some of this anxiety is justified; some isn't. The more you know about child behavior, the less you will worry about many of the normal though not always nice things young children do.

We suggest that the most constructive worrying you might do about any child could take place before he is born or even conceived. Most of us are, fortunately, handing on reasonably good genes. Most of us can reasonably hope that any children we produce will in all likelihood be, if not perfect, at least within a so-called normal range.

But if there are special physical illnesses or behavior abnormalities in the family, some young couples quite wisely ask themselves, are these problems inheritable? What are the chances of their showing up in a succeeding generation?

If you have any anxieties about handing on some dangerous or undesirable characteristic, your best bet is to consult one of the good heredity clinics or genetic counseling clinics now available in many big cities. These clinics do not tell you what you must or must not do. They merely advise you, if either you or the person you are married to has some disease or incapacity, personally or in the family background, about what the chances are of any child you may have inheriting the difficulty. They can also advise you, if you do produce an ill or handicapped child, what your chances are of subsequently producing a normal one.

Couples who are both deaf-mutes, for example, must face the likelihood that any child of theirs will be a deaf-mute. Cerebral palsy, on the other hand, is not hereditary. And the news is also reasonably good for epilepsy. The chances of seizure for the children of an epileptic are estimated at from one in twenty to one in forty. The chance is only one in seventy that such seizures, even if they do occur in the child, will be chronic. These are considered moderate or reasonable risks and the person with epilepsy would thus usually be advised that it is safe to have children.

Much more encouraging traits are those for which *susceptibility* only is inherited. These include such conditions as diabetes, rheumatic fever, and, some think, alcoholism and the malfunction of personality known as schizophrenia. With such illnesses, the environment, or what happens to the organism from the moment of conception till death, largely determines whether genetically susceptible people will or will not develop the difficulty.

Perhaps even more important for parents to know is how safe it is to have a second or third child after producing one severely handicapped child. Serious malformation is highly inheritable. If a woman bears a malformed baby who dies, she has an 11 per cent chance of subsequent malformed children. This is a high risk. However, in the case of many illnesses or abnormalities of a first baby, a heredity clinic will advise that the chances are good of producing a later normal child. Parents need to know what these chances are.

Even if you have been worried but have been given the go-ahead by a heredity clinic, or even (as in most cases) if you have had no special cause to be anxious and have just gone ahead and started a baby, things rarely go seriously wrong in pregnancy. Fortunately, due to a new and remarkable process called amniocentesis, it is now possible for a physician to make a check on the amniotic fluid. Cases of severe abnormality can often be detected through such checking, and in many instances if need be an abortion can be performed.

Thanks to heredity clinics, and to this new method of early detection of abnormality, as well as to constantly improving methods of obstetrical procedure and also to the fact that many people are now limiting the size of their families, an increasing percentage of healthy, normal babies is being born. Another factor which increases a baby's chance of being born with a good physical potential is the increased care young women are taking of themselves during pregnancy. Today there is a greater awareness than in the past of the health hazard to the baby which occurs when a mother smokes, uses drugs, drinks alcoholic beverages, eats an inadequate diet or even suffers from "interpersonal tensions."

Even once your healthy and presumably normal baby has been born, many of you, being parents, are still going to worry about some things. Here are a few of what may be your legitimate worries.

In early infancy, a parent's first justifiable concern may have to do with a child's *feeding*. An occasional spitting up or refusal to take as much nourishment as you think he ought to should not be a subject for concern. But if you absolutely cannot seem to find a formula that agrees, you should consult with, and will need a lot of help from, your pediatrician. Of course, if you breast-feed, as one hopes you may, the likelihood of early feeding problems is reduced substantially.

If early digestive problems turn out to be that fortunately rather rare kind of difficulty known as *celiac disease*, your pediatrician will in all likelihood advise a very special and careful diet.

Colic is a somewhat mysterious malady which strikes young infants especially in the first three months of life. Colic causes parents much discomfort and anxiety. In fact, their own discomfort may exceed that of their infant, even though his intense and prolonged crying may make it seem that he (or she) is in direst agony. Doctors in general believe that the baby himself may not be harmed by his colic. He usually thrives in spite of the loss of sleep and the loss of energy spent in crying.

Relatively little progress seems to have been made either in understanding the causes of colic or in knowing how to prevent it or even how to make the baby more comfortable.

Colic usually starts two or three weeks after birth. One day the baby suddenly turns red in the face; pulls up his little legs and howls. Some believe the difficulty is caused by the baby's swallowing air as he sucks too fast in his struggles to get nourishment. Some believe it is caused by gas. The active bowel becomes blown up like a balloon with gas and when the hard-working large and small intestines find only gas to work on, it hurts. The colicky baby thus may be suffering mostly from gas pains, but he cannot distinguish them from hunger pains and behaves as though he were hungry.

A pacifier may produce some relief. Or, if you place him on his stomach, or over your shoulder, his weight produces pressure on his abdomen that makes him more comfortable. Or you can provide needed warmth with a partially filled hot-water bottle wrapped in a towel and placed under his stomach.

Colic probably occurs most in bottle-fed babies. Many now believe that it is caused by an allergic reaction to something in the formula. In fact, one physician* speaks of a common progression of allergy in children which he calls "the allergic march—from colic to eczema to asthma."

If your baby is being bottle-fed, your pediatrician probably can help you find a formula which will suit. All that may be necessary is to switch from homogenized cow's milk to evaporated milk, or simply to boil the homogenized milk for at least twenty minutes to make the protein elements more digestible. If this simple maneuver is unsuccessful, it may be possible to substitute goat's milk for cow's milk in the formula.

However, we have seen a happy, seemingly healthy and extremely "good" three-week-old breast-fed baby who every evening from six to eight P.M. appeared to suffer painfully, presumably from colic. In such an instance one might suspect that this infant was allergic to something in his mother's milk.

At any rate, diet change for baby if he or she is bottle-fed, for mother if she is breastfeeding her baby, may be one's best plan of attack.

A more serious cause for concern in early infancy is extreme *apathy*. Admittedly heavy babies often move about less than do thin ones. But extreme flabbiness, floppiness, lack of tonus, lack of alert visual regard may sometimes be a sign that your baby is not developing as he should.

One special sign that a baby is not developing properly is persistence of the so-called *tonic-neck reflex* much past twenty weeks of age. The normal four-to-sixteen-week-old baby tends, when he turns his head to one side or the

---

*Dr. Claude A. Frazier, *Coping with Food Allergy* (New York: Quadrangle Books, 1974).

other, to extend the arm on the side toward which he faces, and to flex the other arm. Then, if head turns to the other side, the arm on *that* side extends and the other arm flexes. This behavior normally ceases around sixteen to twenty weeks of age, the child's arm behavior no longer necessarily being related to what his head is doing. A too-persistent tonic-neck reflex much after twenty weeks of age may be an indication that other behaviors as well are not developing normally.

Crying tends to worry new parents, and some babies cry more than others. Dr. Marvin J. Gersh (29) tells us that the average baby may cry about two hours a day. If your baby cries incessantly, something probably is wrong, but it is important not to jump or worry every time crying occurs. Most doctors advise checking to see that nothing is obviously wrong, and if it isn't, accept the fact that normal, healthy babies *do* cry.

Since the time of beginning *creeping* (almost any time from eight months to a year) and of beginning *walking* (almost any time from one year to eighteen months) varies greatly from child to child, if a baby's other behaviors seem reasonably normal, probably most parents do not worry too much about slightly late creeping or walking.

Hand and finger grasp develop so slowly and gradually and through so many substages that in the early months the way your baby grasps objects (or the fact that he fails to grasp) should not and usually does not cause very much anxiety. Even by six months of age most babies usually take hold of objects in a somewhat pawlike grasp. By one year, if not a little sooner, most will spontaneously poke at things with forefinger extended and also will grasp small objects between thumb and forefinger.

Slow *talking* is something that worries many parents a good deal. And even after their child has started to talk, many worry about stuttering or infantile pronunciation. Though the "average" baby probably will utter simple sounds such as "Da-da" or "Mum-mum" by one year of age and will use simple two- or three-word sentences by twenty-one months or two years, keep in mind that the age of beginning talking varies greatly from child to child and tends to be especially late in boys.

Much stuttering or mispronunciation comes under the heading of what is called "preschool nonfluency," and the less attention you pay to it, as a rule, the better. However if either your child's not talking or his odd way of saying things actually bothers you, it is wise to check with your pediatrician or speech clinic just to set your mind at rest.

Any child's *nonsleeping* certainly worries his parents, but it usually bothers them much more than it bothers him. Sleep patterns and amount of sleep needed vary tremendously from child to child. If anything about your child's sleeping or nonsleeping really worries you, check with your doctor. He will probably reassure you that everything is O.K. or, hopefully, will give you the help you need.

Something else that often worries parents is the young child's *fears and terrors.* Neither bedtime fears nor night terrors should as a rule be cause for special concern on the part of a parent. Bedtime fears can usually be dispelled by brushing the imaginary bugs out of the bed, shooing the lion out of the closet, explaining that a fearsome shadow is not really a monster. Or you can provide a night light or a lighted night picture.

The child who wakes frightened from a possibly bad dream can be kissed, cuddled, soothed, fed, and as a rule will go back to sleep. Night terrors do not in most cases indicate that anything is seriously wrong. In fact they are so common around five and six years of age that one almost expects them. However, at least some night waking and expressed distress or discomfort may result either from pin worms, or from foods—especially sweets—eaten at dinner or just before bedtime, to which the child has a delayed adverse response. Conversely, a good protein snack at bedtime may help to prevent the discomfort that can produce night terrors or nightmares, and thus can encourage better sleep.

Other fears should be sympathized with and respected. Fortunately, most people nowadays do not force their child to face the things he fears.

For all these behaviors mentioned so far, assuming that your infant or child seems reasonably bright and alert, for the most part you will do best not to worry. If any special behavior or slowness of behavior or lack of behavior *does* make you anxious, check with your pediatrician. Chances are good that he can reassure you.

Especially late achievement of the *ability to stay both clean and dry* in the daytime inevitably bothers and annoys parents. Parents nowadays tend to be much more patient about toileting, more reasonable in their expectations, than in times past. But even the most patient parent will become understandably restless and even irritated if a three- to four-year-old has not made much progress in either direction.

There is no magic recipe for producing either dryness or cleanliness if they have not come in at the usual times. It may be some comfort to know that if your child is within the normal range, both will be arrived at eventually. When cleanliness is much delayed, especially in a boy, it often is an indication of a personality clash or struggle between him and his mother. Knowing this may help you take off the pressure. It is less fun to fight with a mother who is not fighting back.

So far we've been talking about behavior. Any *physical* problem is something else again. Some children are, admittedly, seriously handicapped by ill health from a very early age. Asthma, allergy, convulsions, epilepsy, cerebral palsy, brain injury or other strongly physically based difficulties should be not so much worried about as checked on. Your doctor will tell you what to do or not to do and will also advise you about whether or not you have real cause for anxiety.

Serious mental or emotional handicaps, too, are something your doctor will advise you about. If your child turns out to be less than normal in intelligence, you will probably wish to join your local branch of the National Association for Retarded Children. You should also read some of the extremely helpful books on the subject, and with the aid of your own physician or school system find out and take advantage of the local facilities that are available for helping and teaching these children.

Less help is available for children who are emotionally ill than for children who are merely less than normal mentally. Your own physician or your local Mental Hygiene Association can generally guide you to a proper source of information about where to get the help you will so sorely need. Now that the psychoanalytic notion that the majority of child problems are caused by parents has been to quite an extent abandoned, you will find that community mental health clinics, available in most cities, can give you substantial and practical help.

The various kinds of mental and emotional disturbances that afflict children are too many and too complicated for us to cover here. But there is one special kind of emotional difficulty we would like to mention briefly.

This condition is known as *autism,* a difficulty characterized by the child's inability to think of or perceive himself as a person, combined with an inability to see others as people and to relate to them.

Such children, though often good-looking or even handsome, and often quite bright, simply do not think of themselves as people (their own name may mean nothing to them) and do not relate to others in the usual way. Thus their mother and father are not special people to them; their nursery-school teacher may be identified by a ring on her finger rather than by her face.

Back in the days when psychiatrists and psychologists still blamed parents for much that went wrong with their children, many believed that autistic children behaved as they did because their parents rejected them. Now, better informed, most of us agree that autistic children behave as they do because of some error in their physical makeup.

Often, though very slowly, these children can be *taught* to relate in a normal, human way to other individuals, though such teaching is usually slow and laborious.

If you fear that you may have an autistic child—that is, if your child is cold, indifferent, almost mechanical in his behavior, with a hollow voice and lack of response to warm, friendly approaches—don't make matters worse by blaming yourself. Your child does not necessarily behave as he does because of something you did or didn't do. Rather, check with your doctor for specific help and advice. And, if you are a reader, read Dr. Bernard Rimland's excellent book, *Infantile Autism* (59). A more recent and extremely helpful book about autism is Carl Delacato's *The Ultimate Stranger* (19).

If your preschooler *is* autistic, probably neither you nor the nursery school will be able to push him into playing with the other children—certainly not right away. But school can help him to enjoy himself *in his own way*. And an effective teacher or nursery-school director can help you in dealing with and living with your difficult child.

One special kind of behavior that some of you may worry about may be partly the fault of the child specialist. It is an apparently ubiquitous condition known as *hyperkinesis* or *overactivity*. Parents of preschoolers often read about this condition and then leap to the quite understandable conclusion that their own preschooler is hyperkinetic.

Keep in mind that nearly all preschoolers (except when

asleep) are almost constantly active. If you think your child is hyperactive, take the opportunity to observe other preschoolers. Chances are you will find that his seemingly constant activity is also quite typical of others his age. (And if your school-age child's teacher tells you that he is hyperactive because he keeps getting out of his seat, remind yourself that it is not unusual for primary-school children to get out of their seats.)

Since most young children *do* move about a great deal more than do most adults, it is extremely important for parents not to confuse a great deal of physical movement with the condition now labeled, among other things, *hyperkinesis*.

Dr. Anthony David, writing in the November 1971 issue of the *Journal of Learning Disabilities,* gives help to parents who may be worrying that their son or daughter may be hyperkinetic. He suggests six areas of behavior that you may think about. From your knowledge and observation of other children, rate your own child as "much less than most children," "less," "slightly less," "slightly more," "more," "much more than most children" for each one of them. Presumably only if your child is over three years of age and still rated as "much more than most" or possibly "more than most," should you come to the conclusion that he really has a problem in this area.

Here are Dr. David's categories:

1. *Hyperactivity.* Is he involuntarily and constantly overactive, always on the move, running rather than walking, seldom still?
2. *Short attention span and poor powers of concentration.* Does he have trouble concentrating or sticking to one thing?
3. *Variability.* Is his behavior unpredictable so that sometimes he is quiet and effective, sometimes extremely active and ineffective?

4. *Impulsiveness and inability to delay gratification.* Does he want everything and want it immediately, thinking only in terms of the present?
5. *Irritability.* Is his tolerance for frustration very low; is he frequently in an ugly mood even when unprovoked? Is he easily upset?
6. *Explosiveness.* Are his fits of anger easily provoked and his reactions almost volcanic in their intensity?

Remember, though, that very young children do tend to show all of these characteristics, so that it is extremely important not to confuse sheer typical preschool constant activity, impulsiveness, and violence of temper with the special *condition* known as hyperactivity.

If you and your doctor do conclude that your boy or girl is truly hyperactive, it is possible that even when he is quite young, you will be advised to use special medication to alleviate the condition. Or as suggested in Chapter 6, you may find that an improved diet will diminish your child's overactivity.

There are perhaps three levels of overactivity. One is the normal almost constant activeness of the ordinary preschooler, especially if he is of a mesomorphic physique. One is the excessive activity of the child known as hyperactive. A third and more serious level of difficulty is known as *brain damage*.

Brain damage is a term widely (perhaps too widely) used to describe children who exhibit marked difficulties in co-ordination control and in adaptation to the usual demands of everyday living in addition to showing many of the characteristics of the hyperactive child. Such children also characteristically exhibit marked errors in perception and in ability to form adequate abstract concepts.

Because of defective perception these children cannot filter out unimportant visual and auditory details. They are bombarded at all times with trivial sights and sounds that compete for their attention. They are forever getting sidetracked. And to make matters worse they do not grasp the wholeness of what they see and hear but perceive only parts. They may concentrate on the metal tip of their shoelaces and forget to lace their shoes.

Because they are not quite sure of their own bodies in respect to size, shape, distance and direction, they frequently trip, fall, and bump into things. They also tend to be destructive and untidy. They never seem still, talking as well as moving incessantly. They have great difficulty socially, since other children dislike their erratic, unpredictable ways.

The best practical help and advice we know of for such children is to be found in two excellent books—Ernest Siegel's *Helping the Brain Injured Child* (62) and Richard Gardner's *The Family Book About Minimal Brain Dysfunction* (27).

Siegel advises that what these children need to help them in their daily living is structure, sequence, and guidance. Above all, keep things simple. Set up routines for every day. Have things take place in a certain standard way and in a certain standard order. Don't vary routines and don't complicate them. And give firm guidance, help, and supervision. The environment must put in the controls that these children lack.

Gardner's book on brain damage addresses itself to the whole family. It explains what brain damage is all about and gives excellent, supportive, and encouraging advice to the brain-damaged child himself as well as to his parents. Either or both of these books provide an excellent place to start in understanding and in helping the brain-damaged child.

And now to conclude, here are suggestions about some other customary and common causes of parental anxiety:

1. Thumb sucking	Don't worry. See pages 113–114.
2. Masturbation	Most child specialists don't worry.
3. Bed wetting before six years of age	Very usual. After that time, if your patience wears thin, try one of the good and inexpensive conditioning devices now available.
4. Child squints, blinks, or complains that he can't see	These behaviors do occur quite commonly around three-and-a-half years of age. Otherwise, for any problems related to your child's eyes or his vision, check with a vision specialist. Also, we recommend a careful vision examination at least every year from the early preschool ages on.
5. Whining	They all do. But whining may mean that the child's day needs to be better planned and more stimulating. Or it may mean that he is not well. Check on both possibilities.
6. Incessant talking	Many do talk incessantly. This is not bad in itself but can be tiring. Giving them a chance to talk into a tape recorder, and then hear themselves, can slightly diminish a constant flow of conversation. And keep in mind that you would be even more anxious if they didn't talk at all.

7. Fighting with siblings

Again, they all do. Your best bet is simply separating them from each other.

8. Allergies

If your child shows allergic reactions to any food, drink, or to any substance in the environment, we urge you to seek the advice and help of a good pediatric allergist. Any uncomfortable kind of behavior, as well as sheer physical difficulties, may be due to susceptibility to certain everyday foods (even foods they like) or to all sorts of pollutants in the environment. Such allergies do not as a rule simply go away and should be taken seriously. (For more detail about allergy, see Chapter 6.)

9. Emotional disturbance as the result of divorce

Most now consider that it is the emotional divorce preceding the legal divorce that most harms the child. In general, people are not advised to stay together "for the sake of the children."

10. Behavior that seems to predict delinquency

It usually doesn't. If you are really concerned, check with a child specialist.

·

12 / Get Help

This chapter will be brief because its message is contained in its title—GET HELP!

There are few things more cuddly and downright lovable than a preschooler. In fact it is undoubtedly their all-round delightfulness that lures so many parents to go on and have others. But it takes a superstrong parent to keep up with one of these often adorable creatures twenty-four hours a day. Of course some of them sleep a little—it hardly seems enough. Even allowing ten or twelve hours out for sleep, a day in the life of the mother of a preschool boy or girl can be long, indeed.

Even if you throw yourself into play with one, with the best will in the world, and even if you let housework and personal life go by the board, by the end of an hour you are likely to have exhausted your resources and your strength, and there are still a good many hours left before bed or naptime.

Taking care of your preschool child will be more of a pleasure and less of a chore if you see to it that you have certain periods away from this charmer. A certain period every day is what we would recommend, a certain period every week at the very least.

Some years ago we spent a month on the coast of Maine with two preschoolers and a baby. The children got up early. The baby-sitter came at nine. Every day we prayed for sunshine and every day we prayed that the baby-sitter would actually arrive. By nine o'clock of any given morning we had used up our combined strength and ingenuity.

You may be stronger, and if you *can* and wish to do the whole thing alone, more power to you. Others among you may be like the twenty-two-year-old mother of two who wrote, "Sometimes I think I got into this whole thing too soon. I don't think I'm ready for it. I don't seem to have the stamina needed. Sometimes I feel like just running away, even though I love my husband and I love my children."

Well, you can't put the clock back, and most of you don't want to. But you *can* get help.

It is important to recognize your own personal tolerances, your limits of energy. You will not enjoy your child or interact with him reasonably if you are overly tired, if you're feeling pushed. This does not mean that you must always be at your best, but it does mean that you should actively avoid being always at your worst.

It takes time and effort but it is wise to sit down with husband, neighbor, friend, relative to assess your own daily limits. Then, as a matter of survival, make breaks in your day when you will get rest, when you can be refreshed by a moment away from the ever constant demands of the preschooler. He is delightful, but not for fourteen or fifteen hours a day. He is not old enough to schedule for your mutual benefit—it will be all up to you.

The ideal situation, assuming that you don't have live-in help (and most people do not), is to have a good, reliable baby-sitter who will come in, not just when the two of you are out for the evening but rather every day or every other day on a regular basis. There is nothing to make a preschooler look better to you than an hour or two away from him. (And especially for those obstinate two-and-a-half-year-olds, or for those tough little four-year-old boys, there's nobody better than a strong, good-natured, ingenious high school boy.)

Some of you may say you can't afford this kind of help. This is something that a grandparent might like to provide. Nowadays many older people prefer to help the young during their own lifetime rather than leaving money in a will, as used to be the custom. Grandparents, for instance, often help with college expenses. They could, if need be, spend a little right now while that grandchild is a preschooler, to assure that he and his mother will live until he gets to college. Just as some grandparents pay for diaper service, some might, if they thought about it, like to pay the baby-sitter.

In addition to or instead of a baby-sitter many young parents have found that nursery-school attendance gives their children desirable extra stimulation and gives them that needed break that turns tiring routine into agreeable and rewarding time together.

A possibly ideal solution is for the child to live mostly at home with a stay-at-home mother, but with those regular and necessary breaks in constant close companionship that can be provided for by a baby-sitter or by nursery-school attendance.

Of course, if you are, like many, a working mother, nobody has to advise you to get help. You have to have it. Fortunately for those many mothers who have to or who prefer to work, there are today many possible alternative ways of providing for the care and comfort of your very young. Some lucky ones do manage to find that treasure, the housekeeper who will live in and take care of the children as well as the house.

Others are fortunate enough to live in communities where day care centers are available for people of all socioeconomic levels, parents paying in accord with their financial ability. A part-time professional mother may even be lucky enough to find a nursery school whose hours coincide with her own working hours.

Sometimes a co-operative neighborhood group of mothers pool their services, to everyone's satisfaction. Fathers often take their turn at child care, especially when parents are still in school.

It isn't always easy to find just the right arrangement, but it usually *can* be done. We urge any mother who does work outside the home not to be burdened by a guilty fear that she is depriving her children of something that is their right—her constant presence. Almost any child, if given the choice, would choose his mother's constant presence, but most child specialists now agree that it is the quality of the mother-child relationship more than the quantity which determines how happy and healthy a child will be.

Happily there are other kinds of help in addition to the physical presence of a sitter, or the physical absence of your child as he attends nursery school or day care center, which are now available for parents.

One kind is the availability of books that now exist, some feel in overabundance, to advise you on any problem which could possibly arise and on some which in all likelihood will never arise. In the Appendix we have listed a few of those that we have found most helpful. There are many others. If you are a reader, and if a good bookstore or library exists in your neighborhood, you will not lack for advice or information on every possible aspect of parenting.

Another tremendous source of help, advice, comfort, and support available is your friendly pediatrician. Pediatricians have always kept babies healthy, but in days not too far past some of them, unlike the earlier family doctor, have not always given as much help as some mothers would have liked. Ask your doctor almost anything about your baby's body—yes. Ask about your baby's behavior—possibly no.

One of Dr. Arnold Gesell's strongest crusades was an attempt to convince pediatricians that "development as well as disease lies in the province of clinical pediatrics." In his opinion, it was as important for doctors to advise parents about their children's behavior problems and difficulties as it was to advise them about their babies' health.

Today a majority of pediatricians can and do give substantial help for all aspects of child raising. And, harking back to the fact that books can help you, several of the most useful books available for parents are authored by pediatricians. We highly recommend: *How to Raise Children at Home in Your Spare Time* by Dr. Marvin J. Gersh (29), *The Children's Doctor* by Dr. Lendon H. Smith (65), and *Infants and Mothers* by Dr. T. Berry Brazleton (10).

Psychologist Fitzhugh Dodson's *How to Parent* (20), *How to Father* (21) and *How to Discipline with Love* (22) will also be of tremendous help.

Another good possibility for getting help is to join or start a parents' group. Former mothers-only clubs have now enlarged in some communities to include fathers, and these gatherings are reportedly increasingly lively. Members meet in small groups on a regular basis to discuss "the problems, joys, and frustrations of raising children—supporting each other—serving as a sounding board—a resource for new ways of dealing with an old situation—group therapy." Meetings are held sometimes with, sometimes without, the children. At some of the meetings, outside speakers provide information on special topics.

There are thus many possibilities. The important thing

is to get some kind of help if all day every day with your preschooler proves to be too much. And don't feel guilty if there are times when you feel that you cannot stand your own child.

Postscript: If, on the other hand, you are a home-bound parent who just loves every minute of every day with your preschooler, by all means stay at home with your child and enjoy yourself thoroughly. Don't get help if you don't want it. But from our observations, it is often sheer physical despair as well as (admit it) boredom and monotony that cause some young mothers to mutter, "Nobody ever told me it would be like this." Just a little rest and recreation is much appreciated by most parents of preschoolers and can do a great deal to help you enjoy and appreciate what can be, with luck, some of the very best years of family living.

13 / School and Your Preschooler

The Typical American Nursery School

Until fairly recently nearly all American nursery schools were pretty much alike in believing that the main thing they had to offer the young child was a chance to play comfortably and happily with other children of more or less his own age and level of maturity in a situation specially geared to his wants and needs. The teachers felt that he should have a chance to express effectively his current abilities, physical, emotional, and social, and should have any help needed in moving on to the next level of maturity.

All of this, in a good school, would take place under the supervision and guidance of kind, friendly adults who understood each child's needs, his abilities and inabilities, and who would take special care not to push him too far or too fast. Such a school can provide not only physical surroundings that are suitable but a daily program geared to the child's level of adequacy.

A good nursery school can help a child develop many aspects of his individuality that may not be tapped or provided for at home. It can provide opportunities for self-expression not always practical at home, and at the same time will in some respects require more adaptation and self control than do home surroundings.

The young child in a good nursery school *has much to learn about himself.* Even though the situation is free and flexible, he does have to adapt to basic rules. This can be quite an eye opener to a preschooler who has been ruling his family with his temper and his demands, as some do. School thus tends to discourage the extreme self-centeredness natural for the young child at home.

School allows the child to experience life away from the protection of his family. It gets him used to the idea of going to school. If he is one who takes separation hard, it will be easier to work out at this level than when he is older.

School encourages self-identity by giving the child a life of his own. It gives him status in his family. It makes it less necessary for him to find excitement through not eating, not sleeping, fighting with siblings, getting into emotional tangles with Mother. Thus school indirectly solves many troublesome feeding, sleeping, and other home problems.

School promotes self-reliance. Here the child can begin to operate on his own. Even the best teacher has less time for him and is less directive than are most mothers. To some extent the child has to think for himself and find his own way. School gives him a certain feeling of independence.

A good preschool allows a child to function where he *is* developmentally, but at the same time gently stimulates him toward a next stage of maturity. But it does not require him to behave more maturely than he comfortably can.

School can help develop a child's language. Sometimes at home, things are provided before he asks. At school he learns to communicate effectively with teachers and with other children.

School may provide exposure to books, art materials and play materials not provided in even a very good home.

In relation to others, there is much to learn. A good nursery school will not worry so much about the child doing things "right" as about his doing them in a way that brings pleasure to him and to others. He will learn, gradually, that certain immediate wishes and demands must be postponed in the interest of others.

Nursery school provides an ideal opportunity for learning to get on with other people—not just with adults or older children who boss him or give in to him but with children of his own age who have the same immaturities, awkwardnesses, and needs that he does. This is one of the most important things a school has to offer. A good teacher will realize that a young child's social self develops slowly and sometimes awkwardly.

Thus she knows that two-year-old children (assuming that they are in school or day nursery at this time) do not as a rule pay much attention to other children. For the most part they engage in what is called parallel play, that is, they play alongside some other child but usually not with him.

By two-and-a-half many children go through a very grabby period when they wish to claim ownership of any toy they have played with, are playing with, or might in the future want to play with. Teachers have to help them share. This can be done by telling them that "Johnny needs that," or "Pretty soon it will be Johnny's turn." Or by asking, "What could we give Johnny to play with instead of the truck?"

By three, many children *are* ready to play co-operatively and can, if necessary, use their own techniques on others, spontaneously offering something they do *not* want in exchange for something they do.

By three-and-a-half a major problem in play may be the child's budding sense of whom he likes and whom he doesn't, so that much playtime is spent in excluding other children: "We don't want to play with you." At this time a teacher's role may be to suggest things that would make the excluded child acceptable: "He's the mailman bringing your mail," or "She's the grandmother, come to visit."

By four most have reached the place where they *can* share and they *can* include, and many now show excellent imagination in play. Teacher's role now may be to set up the playroom with interesting arrangements of furniture or toys, from which children can get their own ideas about *what* and *how* they want to play.

Not only do nursery-school children learn how to share and how to get on with others. They also learn how to handle their bodies effectively. They climb and run and ride their tricycles. They slide and swing and play with big blocks and learn to keep out of each other's way.

Besides improving their own gross motor abilities they also are given a chance to sharpen up fine motor skills. Such efforts are often combined with creative abilities as they paint or finger-paint, play with clay, string beads, dress their dolls, or manipulate all sorts of small play objects.

In a nursery school or day nursery that caters to the very young, the youngest will talk and attend mostly to *themselves,* with only an occasional approach to teacher. By two-and-a-half, though they still are more interested in their teacher than in other children, many now often approach other children, though they may not respond much to others. By three, children attend to other children and to teacher about equally, but now they are beginning to make many responses to the approaches of other children. By four years of age, attention to teacher is only peripheral and occasional. Most of the time is spent in back-and-forth relations with other children.

None of these changes are deliberately taught. For the most part, they depend on the child's own increased maturity. Teachers, rather than actually "teaching" in the conventional sense, teach by providing materials, providing encouragement, providing example. Teachers perhaps do not so much *teach* nursery-school children as play with them, live with them, respond to them, set the stage for them, enjoy them.

Nursery school provides for the preschool boy or girl perhaps the most ideal educational opportunity that will ever be experienced. This is because in nursery school the program is geared directly to the child's abilities. It is flexible enough so that it can change if the group's needs change, and also flexible enough that not all children have to take part at all times or in the same way. In nursery school a child should find a school setting that adapts to him rather than, as at later ages, a setting to which he must adapt.

Nursery school allows for freedom of action. It gives the child a chance to spend time in a physical environment scaled to and planned for him. Here there are not too many things he cannot touch and must not do.

A good school provides not only a wider variety of play materials and play equipment than is available in the ordinary home, but it also provides a variety of experiences, play situations, and excursions that most homes do not provide.

It gives the child a chance to become closely acquainted with a warm, friendly, fostering adult other than parents and close relatives. It provides a situation planned around him rather than one where he is to some extent fitted in, as at home. And it introduces him to the notion of school as an interesting place, where he must conform to some extent but where he can have a good time.

And it helps the child by helping his mother. It not only gives her time away from him but it gives her somebody who knows and likes her child and who will talk over problems and incidents. It gives her clues to ways she might better deal with him. Above all, it helps her by making her child a more independent person.

A Different Kind of School

From the time that we first had preschools in this country until recently there was not much argument or disagreement about what these schools were for. Then came Montessori, and at the same time our government and others began laying great stress on the notion of intervention. Interventionists maintain that if some of our children do not do as well as others in primary school, it is chiefly because they have been deprived at home. They insist that if we could teach them in the preschool years, it could make up for what their home environments lacked.

Interventionists were joined by environmentalists, who believed that you could teach children almost anything at any time, and the sooner you started the better. These influences, and doubtless others, led to the setting up of a kind of preschool in which children did not "just play," but rather worked very hard. Efforts in such schools were directed toward having the children "learn" as academically as possible.

The Montessori movement first came to our shores in the very beginning of this century. At that time Arnold Gesell and other American educators expressed strong reservations about the safety of taking over, without criticism, findings and methods gained from experience with subnormal or environmentally deprived children and transferring them to the normal child. They also pointed out that in their opinion our own school systems do not need the devices, technical apparatus, graduated and systematized processes, and didactic methods characteristic of Montessori. The movement did not catch on at that time.

It appeared again, a few decades ago, and since it fitted in nicely with the educational aims of those who *did* believe that even preschoolers should be taught academically, taught to do things "right," and not waste too much time in mere playing or socializing or growing, it has gained a definite foothold in the United States. Other educators, notably Bereiter and Engelmann, have run even more rigorous preschools, in which young children were very forcibly fed academic materials.

Now that there are two diametrically opposed kinds of preschools in this country, American parents, at least in many communities, are free to choose. They may choose our customary American nursery school in which teachers do not concentrate on reading and writing and matching and following patterns and doing things "correctly," but stress instead the value of play, of gross motor activity, of social experience and expressing oneself as a person, alone or in relation to other children at the behavior level appropriate to the child's own abilities. Or they may choose a more rigorous preschool, in which for the most part academic and fine motor activities are emphasized, and where mostly close work is demanded visually—fine motor activities and close visual work, which we believe the preschooler is not yet ready for.

As a mother who visited one of these more rigorous schools reported, "First they read and then they wrote and then did their bead work and then they matched little designs. I was exhausted just watching them. In one corner, rather inaccessible, was a toy wash basin, and in another a doll carriage and train. It would have taken a highly play-motivated child to demand that the teacher produce either."

Other parents object to the more demanding kind of preschool where the children for the most part work instead of play on the grounds that the quiet, bookish little girls who take nicely to this kind of school actually need to be exposed to more physical and social demands. And the rough, tough, active little boys, who might actually benefit by being calmed down a little, find this degree of rigor far too demanding.

Our vote, obviously, goes to the traditional American nursery school where nobody pushes, where teachers understand and children enjoy at their own age level. No later school situation, no matter how "open" or free, can ever adapt itself to the child's age limitations and his personality demands quite as beautifully as nursery school *if you will let it.* It is an ideal school situation. It seems sad to spoil things by imposing curriculum demands and rigid structure and early emphasis on academics. Particularly so since to this point not only has no one proved conclusively that anything is gained by this early push, but many believe that there is much to be lost.

Ready for Kindergarten

The preschool years get their name, quite obviously, from the fact that they are the years that come before the child starts school. They are, indeed, the years leading up to the beginning of formal schooling. This is important, but it should not overshadow all else. That schooling and academic work will come soon does not imply that these early years, too, should be spent in formal schooling.

One thing the nursery school does *not* do, and is not meant to do, is to make a child ready for kindergarten sooner than he would otherwise have been. A child does not need to learn to read or write or count or even say his letters *before* he starts school, in order to do a good job when he gets there. Conversely, the mere fact that a child does know his letters or can count does not mean that he is *ready* for school.

(If, as well may happen, it turns out that you have an early reader, or an early counter, or a child very advanced with regard to math, all to the good. Do indeed permit him, though do not push him, to express his special interests.)

But many a child will flourish in first grade and in the school years that follow even if there has been no emphasis whatever on academic subjects until the day that he begins first grade.

More important for later schooling than anything you may *teach* him in his preschool years is to be as certain as you can be that before he begins kindergarten or first grade he is actually mature enough to do so.

A New Jersey school superintendent has assured us that if we could persuade parents not to push their children through the preschool years, and then not to push them into kindergarten before they were ready, we would be doing schools, parents, and children a big favor. He commented:

"So many parents today think that because their children have been to nursery school, or have watched *Sesame Street*, and maybe can count, or write their numbers or letters, they are so much more *mature* than children their age used to be, that they are ready to start school much earlier. We had trouble enough with parents whose children missed the entrance cut-off date and who insisted that we allow early admissions. Now with this *Sesame Street* business it's worse than ever."

We, too, have found this; though to balance it we find an increasing number of parents as well as teachers and school administrators who recognize and respect the fact that the time when children begin school should ideally be based on behavior age and not simply on age in years or high intelligence.

Paying attention to birthday age *does* help. If you have no way of getting an evaluation (or making your own evaluation) of your child's *maturity* level, the chances are very good that if he or she is on the older side (fully five for girls, fully five-and-a-half for boys) before entering kindergarten, he *will* make it in school.

A second practical clue to readiness for kindergarten is

if your five-year-old seems to you fully as mature as other five-year-olds of your acquaintance. Also, good clues to school readiness are offered by educators Austin and Lafferty* in their practical and sensible list of things that any parent can check to find out if a child is or is not ready for kindergarten. The full list includes forty-three questions. According to the authors, if you can answer yes to from forty to forty-three, your child is surely ready for school, and if you can say yes to even thirty-five to thirty-nine of them he is probably ready.

We give you here, with the authors' permission, the nine questions from this list that they consider the most significant. If your boy or girl is really ready to start kindergarten, you should be able to answer yes to most of them.

1. Will your child be five years and six months or older when he begins kindergarten?
2. Can he tell you the names of three or four colors that you point out?
3. Can he draw or copy a square?
4. Can he name drawings of a cross, square, circle?
5. Can he repeat a series of four numbers without practice?
6. Can he tell his left hand from his right?
7. Can he draw and color beyond a simple scribble?
8. Can he tell what things are made of, such as cars, chairs, shoes?
9. Can he travel alone in the neighborhood (two blocks) to store, school, playground, or the homes of friends?

Austin and Lafferty have provided a similar list of questions for parents who are asking themselves—Is my child ready for first grade?

Sample questions which should be answered in the affir-

*John J. Austin and J. Clayton Lafferty, *Ready or Not? The School Readiness Checklist*. Published in 1963 by Research Concepts, 349 W. Webster Street, Muskegan, Mich.

mative if the child is ready for first grade include:

1. Will your child be 6 years and 6 months or older when he or she begins first grade and starts to receive reading instruction?
2. Does your child have two to five permanent or second teeth?
3. Can he cut paper with scissors?
4. Can he put together a simple puzzle of six to twelve pieces?
5. Can he tie a knot with a bow?
6. Can he tell his left hand from his right?
7. Can he travel alone in neighborhood (four to eight blocks) to store, school, playground, or a friend's house?

Our own emphasis is that the best criterion for determining when a child should start school should be not birthday or chronological age but behavior age. It is not enough for a child to be five to assure readiness for kindergarten. He needs to be behaving like a five-year-old.

It is important for parents to appreciate that maturity and intelligence tend to be two *separate* measures or qualities. A child may be obviously very bright, that is, very intelligent, and at the same time be immature or young for his age.

Thus saying that a child is immature does not mean that he is not intelligent. We often use the term "superior immature" for that child who is bright but young for his age. The "superior immature" child is one who especially needs protection from the parent or educator who would push him too early into formal schooling just because he *is* bright.

Acceleration in school on the basis of high intelligence, though now fortunately less customary than it used to be, was in days not too far past quite usual. It even had a name —early entrance. The basic notion behind early entrance was this. Mistakenly equating brightness or intelligence with maturity and readiness for schooling, or even totally ignoring the factor of maturity and readiness, many well-intentioned educators made special provision for the child who because of his birthday date, missed the entrance cut-off age.

Say a child was required to be five by October 1 to start kindergarten, and this particular child was not five until October 3 or 4 or 5 or even some time in November or December. Then, even though he was not legally old enough, he was given an intelligence test and if he tested high, was allowed to start school in spite of his chronological youngness.

Early entrance has nowadays been pretty much given up in most communities. This is partly because educators and parents alike have come to realize that being extra bright does not make up for immaturity in producing school success. It has also failed in part because it did not work out very well. As Paul E. Mawhinney* reported some time ago, his community (Grosse Pointe, Michigan) gave it up largely because many chronologically young children who did start school early on the basis of a higher than average I.Q. failed academically. They gave it up partly because parents whose children failed on the test for early admissions tended to become emotionally upset; partly because the added expense seemed unwarranted on the basis of results.

We do not favor the idea of early entrance. Our own preference is that every child before beginning kindergarten should be given a developmental placement, or behavior test, which will tell parent and school whether or not the boy or girl in question is functioning as a full five-year-old (if the class in question is kindergarten) or as a full six-year-old (if the grade in question is first grade).

Though our own test battery includes a certain number of items that check on the child's language ability, to a

*Paul E. Mawhinney, *Michigan Education Journal,* 41, 1964.

large extent our tests help us evaluate the level of those eye-hand coordinations so important in the work that will be required in any formal school situation.

Four of the most significant of our own tests are those which check the child's ability to build with small blocks or cubes, his ability to copy simple geometric forms, his ability to complete a drawing which we designate as the Gesell Incomplete Man, and his ability to perform simple gross motor activities.

Responses to all the behavior tests presented in the Gesell Developmental Battery depend, we believe, on the child's actual level of neuro-motor maturity and not on something that somebody may have taught him or tried to teach him. In fact, the famous California educational psychologist Arthur Jensen* confirms our own findings that it is practically impossible to teach children to copy such forms as a circle, cross, square, triangle, divided rectangle, diamond (the forms we use) beyond the last one in the series they were able to copy without instruction.

Our own school readiness tests are described in a book for parents, *Is Your Child in the Wrong Grade?* (1), and in our most recent book, *The Gesell Institute's Child from One to Six* (3). Here are just a few of the abilities which should have been attained if a child is to be considered ready for pre-kindergarten, full kindergarten or first grade:

4½ Year or Pre-Kindergarten Level:

Makes a five-cube gate from a model
Copies a square recognizably
Adds 7 parts to the Incomplete Man
Hops on one foot

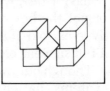

---

*Arthur Jensen, "The Role of Verbal Mediation in Mental Development," *Journal of Genetic Psychology*, 118, March, 1971, p. 63.

5 Year or Kindergarten Level:

Can imitate building of 6 cube steps
Can copy a triangle
Adds 8 parts to the Incomplete Man
Can stand on one foot 9" or more

6 Year or First Grade Level:

Can build a 10 cube step with or without demonstration
Can copy a divided rectangle, 3 lines crossing center line
Adds 9 parts to Incomplete Man
Can stand on each foot alternately

14 / The World Has Changed but Children Haven't

"It's hard to keep up with young people today, they're so much smarter than we used to be at their age."

People often make this excuse for their sometimes less than perfect parenting. But is it true? Are children really smarter?

Better informed? Yes. Healthier? Perhaps. Bigger? Possibly. Smarter? No. Relatively more mature? No.

Vast changes have taken place in our own and our children's worlds in just the past few decades. Air travel is not only routine, but our children have actually seen men on the moon. Computers produce their remarkable results. An atom bomb explodes.

Closer to home, and more intimately, we now have disposable diapers, packaged baby foods, special television programs for children. Smaller families give many a child a quite different home atmosphere from what he might have expected in the not too distant past.

More important to infant and child, however, are the rather dramatic changes in parental attitudes toward children. Since these have come about gradually, many of us do not appreciate what an about-face has occurred in the way most parents think about their offspring.

Within the memory of our oldest citizens is a time when it was considered frivolous to laugh, immoral to sew or to read secular books on Sunday. More recently, adults still viewed children in a very rigorous manner. OUGHTS prevailed. Children ought to be seen but not heard. Children ought to mind their parents. Children ought to behave, ought to tell the truth, ought not to express negative emotions. A child should not say she was nervous because that wasn't a "nice" thing to say.

Most of the rules were made from the point of view of what adults felt would be ideal behavior. Few of them considered what it was reasonable or fair to expect of ordinary children.

Gradually, and little by little, all of this changed. In the 1940's came the notion of self-demand feeding schedules for infants. Babies were no longer required to feed every four hours—mothers adapted their schedules to fit the babies' own internal rhythms.

Toilet training was the next field to be invaded by reason. Instead of virtually competing to see whose baby could be toilet trained earliest, many mothers now relax and take their cues to readiness for training from the child. And in many other fields of behavior parents began to go along with the child's readiness to achieve success rather than with their own determination that he perform in some prescribed manner. The phrase "It's time that—" is heard less often.

Admittedly, some parents, and some specialists, went to extremes. Appreciating that many generations of mothers and fathers had been arbitrarily setting their standards for what their children should do, be, and accomplish and that their demands and punishments had often been unrealistic, some went so far as to take off ALL the rules. In some areas, especially big-city areas, permissiveness flourished. Permissiveness flourished, but children and family living did not.

Fortunately in this instance the pendulum then did not swing all the way back to over-rigorous controls. Many parents settled on a sort of halfway position. They adopted what some have called an attitude of informed permissiveness. That is, they permitted immaturity, but were informed enough about what it was reasonable to expect at any given age to know when to make demands.

In the present era of informed permissiveness many parents are indeed much better informed than parents used to be about what is reasonable to expect of a child at any given age, and of what is reasonable to expect of children with different kinds of personalities.

Now many are going even further than exercising a reasonable patience in waiting for their children to mature to the point where they CAN behave as their parents might prefer. As discussed earlier, many parents are willing for their children, on occasion, to express their quite natural negative feelings—anger, unhappiness, fear. They even permit them to suck their thumbs and fondle their blankets, realizing that children as well as adults sometimes feel tensions that do require an outlet. Even masturbation, a behavior usually distasteful to parents, is gradually being accepted as "normal," though most parents still do not like it.

Parents even go so far, in some instances, as to accept a child's natural curiosity in areas where they themselves may still feel a little sensitive. The excellent book on adoption mentioned earlier, Judith Meredith's *Now We Are a Family*, goes so far as to talk frankly to adopted children about their own natural parents.

Not only has Mother relaxed, but Father's role and relationship to his children has also been changing. Long gone are the days when nearly all fathers followed the pattern described in *Life with Father* of being totally autocratic, monarchs of all they surveyed.

In fact, the single parent family in which the father is that single parent (and thus takes on the responsibilities of double parenthood), though by no means the norm, is no longer unusual. And in many intact families, Father begins to show substantial concern for and interest in a coming baby by taking part in prenatal classes, being present often as "coach" during natural childbirth. Many even speak of "our" being pregnant. Very many, once the baby is born, share diapering, bathing and feeding tasks.

There are some changes in the American family in recent years which unfortunately are not favorable for the children involved. Recent figures give it that one of every eight children in this country now lives in a single-parent home during part of his or her childhood. In 1951 only 600,000 children experienced the breakup of their families through separation or divorce. But by 1976, approximately 2,500,000 experienced the breakup of their family through separation or divorce.

Thus the world in which children are growing up today is in many ways different, very different, from what it was even a few decades ago. Though admittedly some of the changes are not favorable, many, and especially those which affect the very young child, do seem to be definitely to the good. Fathers share more, and both parents tend to be less inclined to push their children toward maturity and perfection. There is more patience with immaturity and with individual difference. Children, being allowed at least to quite an extent to take their own course, and appreciating a more relaxed atmosphere, blossom. Many today in all likelihood are functioning nearer their own optimum level than they might have earlier when things were more tense.

But are the *children* changing? Has there come a change in children equal to the rather tremendous change that has occurred in parental attitude?

In many, though perhaps somewhat superficial ways, children today do seem to be different. Teen-agers seem much more worldly. Five- to ten-year-olds are astonishingly well informed about all sorts of things that years ago were unfamiliar to most adults.

Yet if we consider maturation, or level of development, as opposed to sheer weight of information, the major changes may be rather slight. To us it seems that the major stages of behavior that some thirty years ago we described as being characteristic of the various age levels, still hold. Children still go through the fascinating stages of adoring their parents, later seeing slight and occasional faults, later still finding everything about them totally and discouragingly wrong, and finally, if all goes well, arriving at the stage where the two generations are once again friends.

The major tasks of life—gaining control of one's own body and eventually gaining freedom from one's family and becoming independent—are still carried out in much the same old way.

A specific check to find out whether children are about the same or different in their basic ways of developing has recently been carried out at the Gesell Institute. Results published in *The Gesell Institute's Child from One to Six* (3) are that there has been relatively little change in the past thirty or forty years in the responses of children to the basic Gesell tests.

When responses given in 1940 by children aged two-and-a-half, three, three-and-a-half, four, four-and-a-half, five, five-and-a-half, and six years of age were compared with those given in the 1970's, it appeared that competence was achieved (that is half or more of the children were able to succeed on the test items) at ages that were very similar for the two groups.

Of fifty-one specific comparisons made, twenty-eight, or close to fifty-five percent of behaviors occurred at exactly the same age. In two instances behavior occurred six months earlier in our 1940 subjects. For all other differences, about forty percent, the behavior as measured in the 1970's occurred about six months earlier than in the 1940's.

Just as children today are now on the average larger (reaching full potential presumably because of good nourishment) so they may be slightly advanced behaviorwise. Also, although we attempted to keep the two groups of subjects as similar as possible, some of these differences may have been due to differences in sampling.

At any rate, similarities were more conspicuous than differences. Thus for instance, when it comes to copying a triangle, it is at the age of five-and-a-half years today as in 1940 that the "average" child succeeds. For both groups, it is at four-and-a-half that the child can count to four and respond to the question, "How many?" Or, for our so-called comprehension questions (What should you do when you are hungry? sleepy? cold?) again, understanding seems nowadays to be developing at exactly the same rate as before. Currently, as earlier, over half the children tested are able to answer one question correctly at three years of age, two at three-and-a-half, three at four-and-a-half.

These are, of course, test responses, but in everyday life as well, in spite of the efforts of some to push their preschoolers and accelerate behavior, things don't seem to be too much different from in the past.

Babies still creep when they are around nine months of age, walk somewhere between twelve and fifteen months. A father complained recently that his sturdy thirty-three-month-old son all of a sudden insisted that he be carried everywhere. Father was worried until we suggested that he check in our book, *Infant and Child in the Culture of Today.*

Sure enough, this book tells mothers and fathers that somewhere around thirty-three months of age many little boys and girls go through a period when they like to relive their babyhood. They want their bottle back; they talk baby-talk; they ask to be carried. Though one little girl did tell us, "I'm a baby. I have to have my bottle and I can't walk but I CAN talk."

Two-and-a-half-year-olds still live at opposite extremes, as they did many years ago. The minute they choose blue they want red. Five-year-olds still tend to be co-operative and docile; five-and-a-half-year-olds rude and rebellious. Seven-year-olds still think that everybody is picking on them; eight-year-olds still tend to be overdemanding of their mothers.

Not only do age changes come about much as they always have, but personality still seems to depend very strongly on the way a child's body is built. We still see the tall, thin, sensitive, shy ectomorph; the muscular, sturdy, sure-of-himself mesomorph; the round, friendly, jolly, people-loving endomorph.

Thus our impression is that, especially in infancy and the preschool years, children are developing pretty much as they did in the past. Assuming that the environment does provide adequate food, clothing, shelter, and attention, human beings are probably less influenced by different kinds of environment in the earliest years than in the teen or adult years.

Admittedly, as children grow older, environmental influences play an increasingly important role in determining behavior. Five- to ten-year-olds are today astonishingly well informed about all sorts of things that years ago were unfamiliar even to adults. Teenagers seem more worldly, more selfconfident today.

And as parents relax somewhat their old "Thou shalt not" attitudes toward their children's dating behavior, as they become more understanding about and less afraid of adolescent sexuality, the gulf between adult and older child becomes in many families less wide than it used to be.

But, the basic laws of behavior still hold. Though some

may be able to make out a convincing case in favor of the argument that children are very different from what they used to be, in general we feel that though the world may be changing rather rapidly, young children are probably not tremendously different from what they were twenty or forty years ago.

What about grandparents, one obviously important aspect of a young child's world? It is probably fair to say that some grandparents have changed in many ways and that many have changed in some ways, but that most have changed very little from what they were in the past.

As more older people feel and behave younger than they used to feel and behave, many grandparents have personal lives of their own that may well be more rewarding than in times past. And as relatively more older people give up their family homes for small apartments and condominiums, it is probable that fewer are able to offer that "summer at Grandma's" which used to be traditional for so many.

Probably, though, most grandparents today, even those who dress and live in a highly up-to-date way, feel and behave toward their grandchildren more or less as grandparents have always done.

The majority will probably tell you (and tell you and tell you) that there is nothing like being a grandparent. "I just can't stand it if I don't see him every so often," "Smartest child you ever saw," "Much more fun than our own were because we have all the pleasure and none of the responsibility" are traditional remarks.

Feeling less responsibility, grandparents find it easy to be less anxious, tense, and disciplinary than parents. Somehow they seem to know, better than do most parents, that one slight lapse will not lead to inevitable delinquency.

Children like people who like them, and probably few

people will ever like and appreciate them more than will their own grandparents. Many quite elderly people will tell you that "nobody was ever quite as good to me as my grandmother."

Above all, grandparents, perhaps better than anyone else, are wise enough not to push preschoolers. (An exception here may lie in the matter of toilet training. A few decades ago it was the custom to toilet train much earlier than mothers do now. A few grandmothers, especially those of a bossy disposition, do make life hard for their daughters if they feel these daughters are not pushing hard enough for early toilet training. Their daughters will be wise to ignore their comments.)

In general, though, grandparents tend to be well satisfied with and highly admiring of any and all accomplishments of their beloved grandchildren, however early or late these accomplishments appear. It would be the unusual grandparent who would buy or try to follow any book that would tell how to make a grandchild smarter faster, though we can recommend one book which even the experienced may find helpful—*How to Grandparent* by Fitzhugh Dodson (23).

All in all, the grandparent/grandchild relationship, as almost everybody knows, can be one of the warmest, most satisfactory of any, especially in the preschool years. Grandparents for the most part love, admire, accept, and do not push their grandchildren.

15

Should You Trust the Experts?

Should you trust the experts?

We hope that you do, at least within reason, because there is much that they can do for you. (Since there is considerable disagreement among experts, clearly it is important that you find one whose advice fits in with the things you have observed to be true about human behavior.)

You are fortunate to be living in a day when the specialist can provide good information about both body and behavior. There is much information you need in order to do your very best job of parenting, which only the specialist can provide.

But—you should accept any expert help advisedly. You probably should not trust the experts if they make you nervous, if they are not helpful, if what they tell you goes entirely against your own instincts and feelings and observations about what things work for you and your children.

And especially not if you read them all, so that much of the time you may be getting diametrically opposite bits of advice which do little but confuse you.

Even if you have found some "expert" whose advice you like and which helps you, you should not be *entirely* trusting. Child behavior is by no means an exact science, and many experts change their own advice and opinion from decade to decade.

Though we at Gesell have been highly consistent in the advice we have given to parents over the past half century, even we are not infallible! Take anything you read with at least one grain of salt.

In the final analysis, you and you alone are the expert on your own child. Nobody knows your child and what he is like and what works and does not work with him better than you. And nobody knows *you* and your household better than you. The best advice in the world is not of much help if it tells you to do something that is entirely foreign to your own nature or which just plain would not work in your family.

But we should say that if you have found an expert whose advice in general helps you, seems reasonable to you, is comfortable for you, and works—whether that expert is an expert on the body (your doctor) or an expert on behavior (the psychologist or other child specialist)— then you will be wise to go along with his advice.

Confidence in your specialist can sometimes be of as much help to a struggling, bewildered parent as the actual advice received. Trust is very important. And if on the whole you do not have confidence in either your doctor or your child-behavior expert, you would be wise to seek another.

But don't be a doctor shopper. There are parents who waste their time and money shopping from one doctor to another, hoping to find one who will tell them what they want to hear. What some parents want to hear is that there is really nothing wrong with their child, even when they know in their hearts that there may be something gravely wrong.

Some parents whose children are *extremely* disabled in one way or another tell us that they *have* to shop in order to find *anybody* who will give them even a diagnosis, let alone practical help. If help is hard to find, a parent may indeed find the search a long one. A clue to what you are doing, in such a case, might be to ask yourself honestly:

Am I merely looking for somebody to tell me what I would love to hear, or am I really consulting a succession of doctors in an honest effort to get concrete help and advice?

Admittedly, much contradictory advice *is* given to parents by the different child specialists. This occurs partly because child behavior, or child psychology, is a newer science, and an even more controversial one, than medicine. There is hardly a topic on which all child specialists agree. There are those who tell you that you must breast-feed your baby. There are others who say it doesn't make any difference. Some tell you that it is desirable and safe to use conditioning devices to dry up a wet child. Others say that wetting is merely a symptom of emotional disturbance and that if you dry the child you are merely removing the symptom and covering up the real problem.

Some tell you that if your child is in trouble it is all your fault. Others assure you that most child problems are *not* the fault of the parents. Some tell you that your own efforts can increase your child's intelligence or his maturity. Others tell you that intelligence and maturity are biologically determined and that you can't change them very much.

The main source of argument and controversy among child specialists is based on the old, old argument about heredity and environment. The environmentalists insist that children are like clay, and that it is up to you—and fully possible—to mold them into whatever shape you wish. Those, like us, who have a fuller respect for heredity, believe that the general shape of your child's body and the general shape of his behavior are pretty well determined by genetic forces and that what you can do is always limited by heredity factors.

A current example of these major differences of opinion is found in a book by Arnold Arnold titled *Robbing Your Child of Childhood* (Prentice-Hall). Writes Arnold: "Age grouping in early childhood became popular in the 1940's and 1950's as a result of the wide publicity given the work of psychologist Arnold Gesell. *He contributed, perhaps more than anyone else, to the apprehensions of American mothers* who, Gesell's books in hand, hovered over their children in elation or despair, depending on whether or not their performance coincided with his observations about expected child performance at given ages."

Now here is a good example, and naturally one that we take rather personally, of different points of view among the specialists. Arnold feels that knowing how behavior develops, knowing what to expect, knowing what is normal and what is not, makes people uneasy. Gesell and his colleagues have found that knowing more or less what you can expect, knowing what is and what is not normal, brings peace and confidence to countless parents. (That is why in Chapter 3 we have told you quite a lot about what behavior customarily is like in the preschool years.)

Most mothers and fathers are comforted to find that even many of the peculiar or undesirable behaviors their children exhibit, behaviors that may have worried them unduly, are actually fully normal. In fact, this is what parents from all over the country often say, after reading about usual behavior: "Now I know he's normal. Now I know that *other* children do these strange things, too."

In spite of all the controversy and confusion, there are many situations in which perhaps you should trust the experts, because there is much that they can do for you. They can tell you, within reason, what kinds of behavior you may expect at different ages. This sort of information can help you decide whether or not the behavior you may be worrying about in your child is normal or abnormal.

Even if it is normal, you may not like it and you have every right and reason to try to stop it if you wish. But you won't be quite so worried about some naughty or undesirable behavior if you at least know that most other children go through a similar stage.

Not all of you will be as relieved as the mother who wrote to say: "You have saved my reason." But most people do feel a little relieved to know that their own child is not the *only* one who sucks his thumb, has temper tantrums, snaps back at his parents, refuses to do what he is told, or even lies and swears.

The specialist can also tell you quite a lot about different kinds of personalities. And he or she can help you appreciate that how your child turns out is not *all* up to you. Also, the specialist can keep you informed about new findings in the field of child behavior, and since it is a rapidly growing field, there are many such discoveries.

And lastly, if you do need to seek professional advice, just as a good doctor can examine your child and tell you what is wrong with him and what to do when he is physically ill, so can the child specialist examine your child and tell you what is wrong with him and what to do when his behavior is substantially out of line.

So, our advice would be: if you want to take advantage of the admittedly rather large amount of good solid information about child behavior that does exist, try to find some specialist whose advice you like, whose advice sounds sensible to you, whose advice you feel comfortable with, and then stick with that specialist.

If you are a highly intellectual parent, and enjoy discussion and controversy, you may enjoy reading all you can on *both* sides of any child-behavior argument and then making up your own mind about which suits you best. There is the danger, however, that if you read *all* that is written on both sides of the many heated controversies, you will merely become extremely confused and may quite reasonably conclude that the child specialists don't know what they are talking about and "can't make up their minds."

Appreciate the fact that much basic information about how children grow and what they are like and what you can and cannot do about it is available. And if it helps you to read about such things, get hold of a book or books that present these and other facts clearly and uncontroversially, and then refer to them when you have a problem.

The important thing is that if you read advice which makes you angry, or uncomfortable or which you don't agree with or which doesn't work for you, you don't *have* to follow it. Obviously, no advice is good for you if you don't feel comfortable with it and it doesn't work.

We would even go so far as to say that in spite of all that we have said in this book, if you really want to try to teach your baby or preschooler to read, go ahead. We doubt that it will come to much and we suspect that most of you who try will give it up fairly quickly. But it IS up to you, no matter how negative we may be on the subject.

The experts whom we personally would be the most cautious about trusting are those who report in the popular press that their new "discoveries" show that all former knowledge is incorrect and that you really *can,* by proper efforts, do wonders in changing over your child into something more remarkable than he or she had seemed destined to be.

Even such advice tends not to be fatal. The infant and child, if normally endowed, is his own best protection. We have found, and most of you will discover, that no matter how ambitious or glorious your efforts, hopes and aspirations, most children can be pushed only as far as it is comfortable for them to go, and little further.

Perhaps the child in the long run is his own best expert. He knows what he can do and cannot do even at a very early age. Whatever you may be trying to do, if you meet with a great deal of resistance, you might stop and ask yourself, "Am I trying to go too far, too fast? Am I trying to go in a direction in which this particular child at this particular time is unprepared to move?"

16 / Patience Is Not Permissiveness

Patience, as we recommend it here, should not be equated with either passivity or permissiveness. As one rather firmly disciplinary father expressed it, "If God had believed in permissiveness, Moses would have handed down the ten suggestions." Indeed he might have. And lest any parent believe that what we have been recommending in this book is full-fledged permissiveness, it isn't so.

There are some theories of child behavior so very peculiar, that once they have gone out of style, a new generation can hardly believe that they ever existed. Such a theory was permissiveness, which in its extreme form held that one should never inhibit or thwart a child in any way for fear of the damage it might do to his sensitive psyche.

Most parents who followed this theory were not *entirely* permissive. They permitted more than their own parents had done, but they were still reasonably responsible. Even at its height, permissiveness was not practiced by all parents, and it's probably safe to say that it has been pretty much discarded by most people nowadays.

However, it really did exist and it *does* hang on. One of our own correspondents had this to say:

In your writings you imply that sometimes small children do things that are wrong. By whose standards are they wrong? Who is to say that adults are correct when they consider some children's actions wrong?

With A. S. Neill backing me up, I can say that children should be allowed to do as they like to, and to live out their wants. When they are punished for something they do, they still have an urge to perform the act.

Even though a parent feels that she is helping the child to develop, she is really detrimental to development when she *in any way* suppresses a child's actions.

Most parents and child specialists, even those who at one time were the most ardently permissive, have given up feeling, as this mother does, that one should not in any way suppress a child's actions. Most do, with us, practice or recommend a certain amount of patience, but patience implies neither passivity nor permissiveness. Almost no parent of a preschooler just sits around and allows his or her child to do anything he wishes.

In fact, being patient can be quite as active and can require fully as much energy and know-how as being impatient, probably more. It is easy to shout and slap. It is less easy to arrange your child's surroundings and plan his activities in such a way that they fit in with his needs and abilities.

It is easy to react immediately and violently against whatever it is that your child may be doing. It is less easy to restrain that immediate impulse, to figure out why he did what he did, and to respond calmly and reasonably.

Knowing about what we can and should expect of children of different ages, understanding immaturity and being willing to wait for maturity doesn't mean that a parent should just sit back passively and say of her child, "He's just going through a stage."

Whether he knows what it is reasonable to expect, or not, the ordinary parent will urge, admonish, reprove, and try to *improve* each child's behavior. But knowing what is and what is not normal and to be expected helps you *not* to blame either yourself or your child for immaturities and awkwardnesses.

Knowing what is reasonable also means that though your hopes and goals will remain infinitely high, you will, hopefully, be able to wait. And waiting for a boy or girl to reach some desired stage, to accomplish some desired performance, can be a very active thing indeed. It often takes a good deal of energy to restrain that impulse to push, shove, suggest, insist, and even punish for poor performance or lack of performance.

If you sit idly by because you simply do not care *what* your child does or doesn't do, this might indeed be interpreted as passivity. But if you know what behavior is all about and then in spite of your desire for early excellence, can make yourself wait until the time when it is *reasonable* to expect a certain achievement or success *before* you require it, you are not being passive.

The best parent is not necessarily the one who gets in there soonest with the highest demands and expectations.

But whether you as a parent do or do not know about ages and stages, we live now in a much more realistic and possibly less punitive and "ought-centered" world, so far as children are concerned, than in the past. Thus, fortunately, we are much less likely nowadays to say, "It's time that" my child did this or that—meaning merely that we are tired of waiting for the behavior, rather than that we really know it *is* time for it to occur.

As noted earlier, we no longer are as likely as in the past to say that a child must give up the "bad habit" of sucking his thumb. Today we ask ourselves, instead, why does he need this tension outlet? How can we make him so comfortable that he may not need it? How does he feel about it?

Knowing about ages does not mean that you simply sit back and wait. Similarly, knowing about constitutional psychology and understanding and respecting the kinds of behavior characteristic of children of different physical types doesn't mean that you merely sit back and say, "She's terribly shy, but what else can you expect from an ectomorph?"

Knowledge of either stages or personality types means that you use this knowledge to guide you about what is reasonable and not reasonable to expect, and about what you can and cannot do to help your child comport himself most comfortably and effectively.

Many parents today seem to us to do a very good job of steering a fair middle course between being overstrict and overpermissive, but some still will find, if they check on themselves, that they may almost automatically say "no" to most or many requests that their younger children make. "Mummy, may I play with the sprinkler?," "Mummy, may I have a snack?" Some things, certainly, do need to be forbidden, but many others *could* be allowed without so very much damage to either property or discipline.

Even though it may take some effort to check your automatic "no," try before you say it to give your child's request at least a second thought, a fair consideration. (An automatic "no" may do as much harm to good discipline as an automatic "yes.")

Being patient, giving your child's request a second thought, is an active, not a passive response on your part. Giving in to a reasonable request does not constitute permissiveness.

So, let us say once more, you do not need to push your preschooler. Patience really will pay off. Your life with the very young child, though sometimes physically taxing, should not be a thing of effort and struggle. The enthusiasm of the preschooler, his love of life, his admiration of you can make him a most rewarding companion if you will just relax and enjoy him.

Then, don't you need to teach your child anything? Of course you do! You teach every day if not every hour. You teach by what you say, by what you do, by what you are. You teach him and lead him and show him and explain things to him. You provide new sights and sounds and situations. You set up his day and his life so that it will be comfortable but at the same time stimulating and rewarding.

You do all these things, but we still maintain, you should not push. And *whatever* you do should be highly individual. Always remember that no matter what you do, no matter how many books you provide, how many toys, how much lively conversation, not every child will turn out to be a genuine scholar. Some children are much better at living than they are at formal learning.

Nature's blueprints are highly individual. If or when a child does not turn out to be a real "learner," does not get good grades in school, or even like school so terribly much, you must not feel that YOU are to blame because you are not doing the right things for him, or didn't do the right things in his preschool years.

No, you do not need to push. And, hopefully, you will not confuse patience with passivity. Try to keep in mind that a biological point of view, which holds that each individual has his or her own timetable, does not mean that there is nothing that you and the rest of the environment can do.

It does mean that the environment will do what it does much more effectively if it is working within known and realistic limits rather than pushing to make a child into something that biology never intended. You will have the greatest success if you do not try to speed your child into behavior that a still young body is not ready to perform.

Respect individuality. Respect immaturity. Respect your child for what he or she is now, as a preschooler. There may never be a happier time.

Appendix:
Books for Parents

If you are the parent of even one preschooler, chances are you may not have vast amounts of time or energy for reading.

Still, that active dynamo of yours does eventually get to bed—if not to sleep. In fact, if you are lucky, he or she still will accept at least a play nap in the afternoon. So the moment may come, now and then, when you do get a chance to read.

Useful books about child behavior can, ideally, not only inform and instruct you. Some may even amuse. Others may help to solve your own special problems. Still others can support and reassure. Many parents have reported through the years that reading about the way *other* children behave is a vast relief. "Now I know he's not the *only* one," or "Now I know he's normal," they tell us.

Good books for parents are so numerous these days that it is difficult to choose the very best. But here are seventy or so of those we have found the most useful.

1. Ames, Louise B. *Is Your Child in the Wrong Grade?* Lumberville, Pa.: Modern Learning Press, 1978.
2. Ames, Louise B. *Child Care and Development,* rev. ed. Philadelphia, Pa.: Lippincott, 1979.
3. Ames, Louise B.; Gillespie, Clyde; Haines, Jacqueline; and Ilg, Frances L. *The Gesell Institute's Child from One to Six.* New York: Harper & Row, 1979.
4. Ames, Louise B., and Ilg, Frances L. *Your Two Year Old: Terrible or Tender?* New York: Delacorte, 1976.
5. Ames, Louise B., and Ilg, Frances L. *Your Three Year Old: Friend or Enemy?* New York: Delacorte, 1976.
6. Ames, Louise B., and Ilg, Frances L. *Your Four Year Old: Wild and Wonderful.* New York: Delacorte, 1976.
7. Ames, Louise B., and Ilg, Frances L. *Your Five Year Old: Sunny and Serene.* New York: Delacorte, 1976.
8. Bley, Edgar S. *Launching Your Preschooler.* New York: Sterling Press, 1955.
9. Braga, Laurie, and Braga, Joseph. *Learning and Growing: A Guide to Child Development.* Englewood Cliffs, New Jersey: Prentice Hall, 1975.
10. Brazleton, T. Berry. *Infants and Mothers.* New York: Delacorte, 1969.
11. Brazleton, T. Berry. *Toddlers and Parents.* New York: Delacorte, 1974.
12. Calladine, Andrew, and Calladine, Carole. *Raising Siblings,* New York: Delacorte, 1979.

13. Caplan, Frank, and Caplan, Theresa. *The Power of Play.* New York: Doubleday, 1973.
14. Chess, Stella; Thomas, Alexander; and Birch, Herbert. *Your Child Is a Person.* New York: Viking, 1965.
15. Comer, James P., and Pouissant, Alvin F. *Black Child Care.* New York: Simon & Schuster, 1975.
16. Crain, William C. *Theories of Development.* Englewood Cliffs, New Jersey: Prentice Hall, 1979.
17. Crook, William G. *Can Your Child Read? Is He Hyperactive?* Jackson, Tennessee: Pedicenter Press, 1975.
18. Crook, William G. *Tracking Down Hidden Food Allergy.* Jackson, Tennessee: Professional Books, 1978.
19. Delacato, Carl. *The Ultimate Stranger: The Autistic Child.* New York: Doubleday, 1974.
20. Dodson, Fitzhugh. *How to Parent.* Los Angeles: Nash, 1970.
21. Dodson, Fitzhugh. *How to Father.* Los Angeles: Nash, 1974.
22. Dodson, Fitzhugh. *How to Discipline with Love.* New York: Rawson, 1977.
23. Dodson, Fitzhugh. *How to Grandparent.* New York: Lippincott, 1980.
24. Doman, Glenn. *Teach Your Baby Math.* New York: Simon & Schuster, 1980.
25. Edwards, Vergne. *The Tired Adult's Guide to Backyard Fun.* New York: Crowell, 1957.
26. Feingold, Ben. *Why Your Child Is Hyperactive.* New York: Random House, 1975.
27. Gardner, Richard A. *The Family Book About Minimal Brain Dysfunction.* New York: Aronson, 1973.
28. Gardner, Richard A. *Understanding Children.* New York: Aronson, 1973.
29. Gersh, Marvin J. *How to Raise Children at Home in Your Spare Time.* New York: Stein & Day, 1966.
30. Gesell, Arnold; Ilg, Frances L.; and Ames, Louise B. *Infant and Child in the Culture of Today,* rev. ed. New York: Harper & Row, 1974.
31. Gesell, Arnold; Ilg, Frances L.; and Ames, Louise B. *The Child from Five to Ten,* rev. ed. New York: Harper & Row, 1977.

32. Ginott, Haim. *Between Parent and Child.* New York: Macmillan, 1965.
33. Grollman, Rabbi Earl, ed. *Explaining Death to Children.* Boston: Beacon Press, 1967.
34. Grollman, Rabbi Earl, ed. *Explaining Divorce to Children.* Boston: Beacon Press, 1969.
35. Grollman, Rabbi Earl. *Talking About Death: A Dialogue Between Parent and Child.* Boston: Beacon Press, 1976.
36. Harrison-Ross, Phyllis, and Wyden, Barbara. *The Black Child: A Parent's Guide.* New York: Peter Wyden, Inc., 1973.
37. Hatfield, Antoinette K., and Stanton, Peggy S. *How to Help Your Child Eat Right.* Washington, D.C.: Acropolis Books, 1978.
38. Hedges, William D. *At What Age Should Children Enter First Grade?* Ann Arbor, Michigan: University Microfilms International, 1977.
39. Holt, John. *How Children Fail.* New York: Pitman, 1964.
40. Hoopes, Ann, and Hoopes, Townsend. *Eye Power.* New York: Knopf, 1979.
41. Ilg, Frances L.; Ames, Louise B.; and Baker, Sidney M. *Child Behavior,* rev. ed. New York: Harper & Row, 1981.
42. Ilg, Frances L.; Ames, Louise B.; Haines, Jacqueline; and Gillespie, Clyde. *School Readiness,* rev. ed. New York: Harper & Row, 1978.
43. Jones, Hettie. *How to Eat Your ABC's: A Book About Vitamins.* New York: Four Winds Press, 1976.
44. Kelly, Marguerite, and Parsons, Elia. *The Mother's Almanac.* New York: Doubleday, 1975.
45. Kohl, Herbert. *Growing with Your Children.* Boston: Little, Brown, 1979.
46. Kraskin, Robert A. *You Can Improve Your Vision.* New York: Doubleday, 1968.
47. Lansky, Vicki. *The Taming of the C.A.N.D.Y. Monster.* Wayzata, Minnesota: Meadowbrook Press, 1978.
48. Levine, Milton L., and Seligmann, Jean E. *The Parents' Encyclopedia of Infancy, Childhood and Adolescence.* New York: Crowell, 1973.

49. Lief, Nina. *The First Year of Life: A Curriculum for Parenting Education.* New York: Keyway Books, 1979.
50. Liepmann, Lise. *Your Child's Sensory World.* New York: Dial, 1973.
51. Liley, Margaret, with Beth Day. *Modern Motherhood: Pregnancy, Childbirth and the Newborn Baby.* New York: Simon & Schuster, 1964.
52. Maynard, Fredelle. *Guiding Your Child to a More Creative Life.* New York: Doubleday, 1973.
53. McCoy, Elin. *Fun with Sun, Shade, Water, Wind and Snow.* New York: Random House, 1979.
54. McIntire, Roger W. *For Love of Children.* Del Mar, California: CRM Books, 1970.
55. Painter, Genevieve. *Teach Your Baby.* New York: Simon & Schuster, 1972.
56. Patterson, Gerald R. *Families: Applications of Social Learning to Family Life.* Champaign, Illinois: Research Press, 1971.
57. Pitcher, Evelyn G., and Ames, Louise B. *The Guidance Nursery School.* New York: Harper & Row, 1974.
58. Ramos, Suzanne. *The Complete Book of Child Custody.* New York: G. P. Putnam's Sons, 1979.
59. Rimland, Bernard. *Infantile Autism.* New York: Appleton-Century-Crofts, 1963.
60. Samuels, Mike, and Samuels, Nancy. *The Well Baby Book.* New York: Summit, 1979.
61. Sheldon, William H. *The Varieties of Temperament.* New York: Hafner, 1970.
62. Siegel, Ernest. *Helping the Brain Injured Child.* New York: New York Association for Brain Injured Children, 1961.
63. Siegel, Ernest; Siegel, Rita; and Siegel, Paul. *Help for the Lonely Child.* New York: Dutton, 1978.
64. Skoussen, W. Cleon. *So You Want to Raise a Son.* New York: Doubleday, 1962.
65. Smith, Lendon H. *The Children's Doctor.* Englewood Cliffs, New Jersey: Prentice Hall, 1969.
66. Smith, Lendon H. *Improving Your Child's Behavior Chemistry.* Englewood Cliffs, New Jersey: Prentice Hall, 1976.

67. Smith, Lendon H. *Feed Your Kids Right.* New York: McGraw Hill, 1979.
68. Smith, Robert Paul. *How to Grow Up in One Piece.* New York: Harper & Row, 1963.
69. Sparkman, Brandon, and Carmichael, Ann. *Blueprint for a Brighter Child.* New York: McGraw-Hill, 1973.
70. Stevens, Laura J., and Stoner, Rosemary. *How to Improve Your Child's Behavior Through Diet.* New York: Doubleday, 1979.
71. Stewart, Mark A., and Olds, Sally W. *Raising a Hyperactive Child.* New York: Harper & Row, 1973.
72. Thompson, Helen. *The Successful Step-Parent.* New York: Harper & Row, 1968.
73. Von Hilsheimer, George. *How to Live with Your Special Child—A Handbook for Behavior Change.* Washington, D.C.: Acropolis Press, 1970.
74. Wenar, Charles. *Personality Development from Infancy to Adulthood.* Boston, Mass.: Houghton Mifflin, 1971.
75. Wender, Paul H. *The Hyperactive Child: A Handbook for Parents.* New York: Crown, 1973.
76. White, Ruth Bennett. *Food and Your Future.* Englewood Cliffs, New Jersey: Prentice Hall, 1979.
77. Wunderlich, Ray. *Allergy, Brains and Children Coping.* St. Petersburg, Florida: Johnny Reads Press, 1973.

Index